HOLLYWOOD

·HOLLYWOOD BABYLON·

Every Man and every Woman is a Star.
—Aleister Crowley

HOLLYWOOD

BABYLON

by
Kenneth
Anger

Distributed by
Simon and Schuster
Order number: 21979

Design direction: Tony Lane
Book design: Kenneth Anger

Library of Congress Card Catalog
Number: 74-18226
ISBN: 0-87932-086-9

Typesetting: Timely Typography
Printed in the United States of America
by Kingsport Press 10 9 8 7 6 5 4

Straight Arrow Books
625 Third Street
San Francisco, California 94107

Published by arrangement with the
Stonehill Publishing Company.

To
the Scarlet
Woman

· CONTENTS ·

HOLLYWOOD

Hollywood, Hollywood . . .
Fabulous Hollywood . . .
Celluloid Babylon,
Glorious, glamorous . . .
City delirious,
Frivolous, serious . . .
Bold and ambitious,
And vicious and glamorous.
Drama — a city-full,
Tragic and pitiful . . .
Bunk, junk, and genius
Amazingly blended . . .
Tawdry, tremendous,
Absurd, stupendous;
Shoddy and cheap,
And astonishingly splendid . . .
HOLLYWOOD!!

     — Don Blanding

(As recited by Leo Carillo in the 1935 MGM
Colortone Musical, Star Night at the
Cocoanut Grove.)

· THE PURPLE DAWN ·

WHITE ELEPHANTS — the God of Hollywood wanted <u>white elephants,</u> and white elephants he <u>got</u> — eight of 'em, plaster mammoths perched on mega-mushroom pedestals, lording it over the colossal court of Belshazzar, the pasteboard Babylon built beside the dusty tin-lizzie trail called Sunset Boulevard.

Griffith — the Movie Director as God — was riding high, high as he'd ever go, over Illusion City, whooshing up a hundred-foot high elevator camera tower, giant megaphone poised to shout the command to the thousands below, the CAMERA-AH ACTION-N-N! to bring it all alive. . . .

Belshazzar's Feast beneath Egyptian blue skies, spread out under the blazing Southern California morning sun: more than four thousand extras recruited from L.A. paid an unheard-of two dollars a day plus box lunch plus carfare to impersonate Assyrian and Median militiamen, Babylonian dancers, Ethiopians, East Indians, Numidians, eunuchs, ladies-in-waiting to the Princess Beloved, handmaidens of the Babylonian temples, priests of Bel, Nergel, Marduk and Ishtar, slaves, nobles and subjects of Babylonia.

<u>Griffith's Vision of Babylon!</u>

A mare's nest mountain of scaffolding, hanging gardens, chariot-race ramparts and sky-high elephants, a make-believe mirage of Mesopotamia dropped down on the sleepy huddle of mission-style bungalows amid the orange groves that made up 1915 Hollywood, portent of things to come.

The Purple Epoch had begun.

And there it stood for years, stranded like some gargantuan dream beside Sunset Boulevard. Long after Griffith's great leap into the unknown, his Sun Play of the Ages, <u>Intolerance</u>, had failed; long after Belshazzar's court had sprouted weeds and its walls had begun to peel and warp in abandoned movie-set disarray; after the Los Angeles Fire Department had condemned it as a fire hazard, still it stood: Griffith's Babylon, something of a reproach and something of a challenge to the burgeoning movie town — something to surpass, something to live down.

The shadow of Babylon had fallen over Hollywood, a serpent spell in code cuneiform; scandal was waiting, just out of Billy Bitzer's camera range.

Hollywood, the movie colony, had been forged into existence by a small group of East Coast Jewish tradesmen who thought they saw a good thing in the nickelodeon, lured West by that fabled

← Illusion City's Elephants   Belshazzar's Feast →

Southern California promise of 355 days of sunshine a year, and low-priced land. The somnolent L.A. outpost in the orange groves they settled on soon sprouted ramshackle open-air stages, sun traps for their slow ortho film. In a few years of churning out primitive and profitable two-reelers with their pirated cameras — always on the lookout for Edison's vengeful process servers — the former junk dealers and glove salesmen juggled a chancy operation into a celluloid bonanza.

When word reached them that nickelodeon crowds all over the country seemed to be flocking to see favorite movie performers known only as "Little Mary," "The Biograph Boy" or "The Vitagraph Girl," the disdained actors, until then thought of as little more than hired help, suddenly acquired ticket-selling importance. The already-famous faces took on names and rapidly-rising salaries: the Star System — a decidedly mixed blessing — was born. For better or for worse, Hollywood would henceforth have to contend with that fatal chimera — the STAR.

Overnight the obscure and somewhat disreputable movie performers found themselves propelled to adulation, fame and fortune. They were the new royalty, the Golden People. Some managed to cope and took it in their stride; some did not.

The Teens were Hollywood's halcyon days. A new art form was being forged from day to day; the Seventh Muse made herself up as she went along, making money and having fun. And if the nouveau riche film folk got tired from the furious pace, there was always "joy powder," as cocaine was called in those free-and-easy days, for a sure-thing pick-you-up. In fact, a "joy powder" manic movie comedy style rapidly evolved — the prime example being the Triangle-Keystone "cokey comedy," The Mystery of the Leaping Fish, with Doug Fairbanks as a bombed-out-of-his-skull detective, "Coke Ennyday." In 1916 "dope" could be the subject of comedy. The year of that film, The Mystery of the Leaping Fish, English drug expert Aleister

"Ruins" of Babylon in 1919 ↑

Theda Bara: First Sex Queen →

6

Crowley passed through Hollywood, taking note of the natives as "the cinema crowd of cocaine-crazed, sexual lunatics." Those were the days.

Gossip there was, as among any group of show folk, but as yet unenshrined in the newspaper column: Louella O. Parsons had yet to set up shop. Behind the scenes, among themselves, the miniature movie colony even dared to gossip about the God of Hollywood — Griffith's obsession, on screen and off, with young, female children. And were those Griffith discoveries, those devoted, hard-working child–women, really all that virginal? Was it possible? And, thinking the unthinkable, was Lillian Gish Dorothy's lover?

But it was harmless, really, even the speculations about Richard Barthelmess posing for "French postcards" when he was trying to make his way or the more solid speculations about Mack Sennett's famous "Bathing Beauty" casting couch . . . the original model of a long line. If some liked to think of Sennett's Sunshine Girls, including such buds as teenage Gloria Swanson and Carole Lombard, as a hand-picked harem, why, that didn't bother Big Mack. Theda Bara was always good for a laugh. The colony knew that the fatal vamp, being sold to the rubes as a French-Arab demon of depravity born beneath the Sphinx, was in truth Theodosia Goodman, a Jewish tailor's daughter from Chillicothe, Ohio, a meek little goody-two-shoes.

In a few more years America's

← Theda in Salome: Gossip there was   Lillian and Dorothy Gish: Lovers? ↑   Hollywood:Babylon →

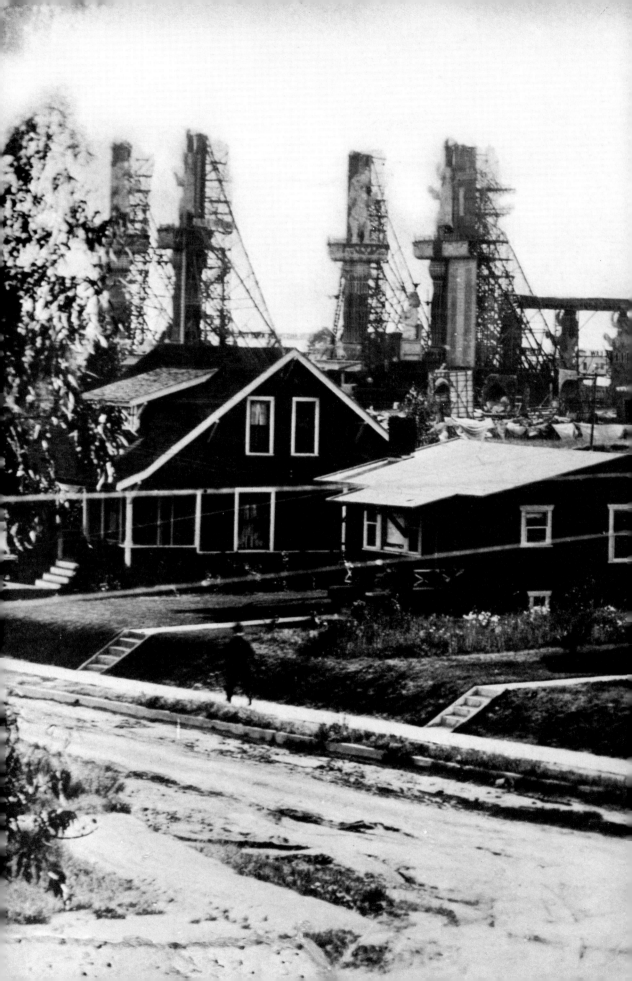

self-righteous preachers would be maligning the movie colony and all its works; Hollywood, California became a synonym of Sin. Professional do-gooders would brand Hollywood a New Babylon whose evil influence rivaled the legendary depravity of the old; banner headlines and holier-than-thou editorials would equate Sex, Dope and Movie Stars. Yet while the country's organized cranks screamed for blood and boycott, the public, unfazed, flocked to the movies in ever-increasing multitudes.

The Twenties is sometimes referred to as "Hollywood's Golden Age," and golden it was, in sheer exuberant movie-making creativity as well as in financial returns. Film folk of the period are depicted as engaging in madcap, nonstop off-screen capers. The legend overlooks one fact — fear. That ever present thrilling-erotic fear that the bottom could drop out of their gilded dreams at any time.

Scandals exploded like time bombs throughout the delirious decade of "Wonderful Nonsense," as screen career after career was destroyed. Each star wondered if it was his turn to be the next scapegoat. For Hollywood the fabled "Golden Age" was more like a lavish picnic on a shaky precipice; the road to glory was beset with booby traps.

Yet for the vast public out there H-O-L-L-Y-W-O-O-D was a magic three syllables invoking the Wonder World of Make Believe. To the faithful it was more than a dream factory where one young hopeful out of a million got a break. It was Dreamland, Somewhere Else; it was the Home of the Heavenly Bodies, the Glamor Galaxy of Hollywood!

The fans worshipped, but the fans also could be fickle, and if their deities proved to have feet of clay, they could be cut down without compassion. Off screen a new Star was always waiting to make an entrance.

Theda: Synthetic Sin ↑

"Early Egyptian" Movie Temple →

·THE CLUTCHING HAND·

A cloud, no larger than a girl's hand, was taking shape on the horizon.

The shocking news that first revealed Hollywood in a scandalous light arrived on September 10, 1920 in the form of a Marconi Radiogram that waked Myron Selznick in the middle of the night. The message made front page headlines:

OLIVE THOMAS DEAD
FROM POISON
Olive Thomas, sprightly Ziegfeld
Follies' queen,
Selznick Pictures star and
Mrs. Jack Pickford . . .

The cablegram informed the head of Selznick Pictures that his top star had just been found dead in Paris.

The sedate, renowned Hotel Crillon, on the Place de la Concorde, was a most unlikely setting for Hollywood's first scandal. On that September morning the valet used his passkey to enter the hotel's Royal Suite with a breakfast trolley. What he saw froze him in his tracks. A sable opera cape was spread out on the floor, and on it lay a nude young woman. One hand still clutched a bottle of toxic bichloride of mercury granules. The suite was registered in the name of Mrs. Jack Pickford, known to millions of

adoring fans as the bright young star of the silver screen, Olive Thomas.

Olive Thomas! New York remembered her as one of the most beautiful brunettes Ziegfeld had ever glorified. Ziegfeld's showgirls were invariably young, and at sixteen Olive was a poised, vivacious young lady much sought after by café society, darling of the Vogue and Vanity Fair crowd, ornament of the penthouse parties given by the publisher of those modish magazines, Condé Nast. Through the ministrations of Mr. Nast, Olive had appeared frequently as a fashion model in the pages of Vogue, and Mr. Ziegfeld singled her out to pose, unclothed, for the young Peruvian artist, Alberto Vargas. The artist Harrison Fisher called Olive "the most beautiful woman in the world." Her subsequent departure for Hollywood seemed only natural.

The bubbly beauty from Broadway "caught on" at once in the film colony, and her pert portrayals of young girlhood in light comedies like Betty Takes a Hand, Prudence on Broadway and — inevitably — The Follies Girl, swiftly won her a wide following. In 1919 Myron Selznick launched his newly formed company by signing Elaine Hammerstein and Olive Thomas to lucrative contracts. In 1920, with Olive's success

---

← Olive Thomas: Picture of Innocence

in The Flapper and her much publicized marriage to Jack Pickford, Mary Pickford's brother and himself an idol of the screen, her place in the charmed circle of Golden People seemed assured.

The suicide of Olive Thomas made headlines around the world and touched off furious controversy. Olive was just twenty when she died; she had youth, beauty, wealth, fame and love, and not only the adulation of her fans but the adoration of Jack Pickford. Young Jack had been characterized as the "Ideal American Boy" in such films as Seventeen, Olive as the "Ideal American Girl" in The Tomboy. They were portrayed in the new fan magazines as "The Ideal Couple." What could have made Olive Thomas kill herself?

Olive's studio, whose slogan was "Selznick Pictures Create Happy Homes," was deluged with letters; the American Embassy in Paris and the French police promised complete investigations.

What the investigations of Olive's death disclosed, and the papers headlined, was a lurid private life that did not tally at all with her Hollywood image as a sweet young thing. Jack Pickford had been due to join Olive in Paris as soon as he completed work on The Little Shepherd of Kingdom Come. They had planned on a Paris idyll to make up for the honeymoon which picture-making had prevented right after their marriage. Olive had gone on ahead to shop for antiques and clothes, but it was disclosed that her perambulations had not all been directed to the chic salons. She had been seen night clubbing at the Jockey and the Maldoror with some notorious figures of the French underworld; she had sought out some of the roughest, meanest dives of Montmartre.

A story began to circulate about the motivation for Olive's plunge into the Parisian bas-fonds: she was desperately trying to score a large quantity of heroin to supply her husband, Jack, who was a hopeless addict. Failing this, she had committed suicide.

When this story appeared in the American press, Jack was under treatment for nervous collapse following the news of his wife's death and could not refute the charges. His loyal sister Mary, just emerging from the controversy of double divorce and marriage to Doug Fairbanks, took it upon herself to issue a statement from her new domain, Pickfair, denying such "sickening aspersions" on her brother's character. Shortly thereafter, an investigation conducted by the United States Government into the activities of a certain Captain

Olive and Jack: "Ideal Couple" ↑   Olive in Hollywood →

16

Spaulding of the United States Army who had been arrested for dealing in cocaine and heroin on a large scale, revealed in his little black book of steady clients the name of the erstwhile "Ideal American Girl."

OLIVE THOMAS, DOPE FIEND!

Thus the headlines described lovable "kid sister" Olive — and it was a shock. In 1920 most of America still paid lip service to Victorian morality. Watch and Ward societies began to speak out about the new menace to American maidenhood, and Chicago's Cardinal Mundelein felt called upon to issue a tract entitled The Danger of Hollywood: A Warning to Young Girls.

With the Twenties the upstart film capital was luring trainloads of young hopefuls from all over the land. Some were local beauty contest winners; most were merely pretty, plucky and poor. All wanted to be movie stars, but few of them even found work as extras, or "atmosphere." For thousands it was a trip to Heartbreak City.

The sensational death of Olive Thomas caused another star's suicide that September of 1920 to pass almost unnoticed. Bobby Harron, the sensitive "Boy" of Intolerance, shot himself in a New York hotel room on the eve of the premiere of Way Down East. Griffith had bypassed Bobby for that film, preferring his new favorite, Richard Barthelmess. It broke Bobby's heart.

It was Olive's death that was "made to order" for the sob sisters of the day, who loaded the tabloids with morbid speculation. Olive Thomas was good copy for a year following her death, until one of those "young Hollywood hopefuls" crowded her out of the headlines: a rather minor actress, a pal of roly-poly comic Fatty Arbuckle.

Olive Thomas's Last Hours in Paris

Olive's death: Good copy ↑

Olive: The Tomboy →

· FAT MAN OUT ·

Roscoe "Fatty" Arbuckle was a hefty plumber's helper discovered by Mack Sennett in 1913 when he came to unclog the comedy producer's drain. Sennett sized up the affable, 266-pound Roscoe and offered him a job on the spot. Arbuckle's butterball appearance and bouncing agility were perfect foils for Sennett's brand of film farce — mud and mayhem, pratfalls and custard pies.

Working his way up from the Keystone Cops, Fatty went on to team with Mabel Normand in Fatty's Flirtations, Charlie Chaplin in The Rounders, Buster Keaton in The Butcher Boy and other popular two-reel comedies. Fatty's natural talent as a jovial jackanapes assured his success as a screen buffoon and made his fortune.

Fatty's value as a laugh-maker rocketed his Sennett three-dollar-a-day salary of 1913 to $5000 a week in 1917, when he signed with Paramount. A "gag" banner over the famous gate proclaimed: PARAMOUNT WELCOMES THE PRINCE OF WHALES.

The boozy all-night revel held on March 6 at Mishawn Manor, Boston, to celebrate that signing almost became a public scandal. It took place at Brownie Kennedy's Roadhouse, where the lavish entertainment laid on in Fatty's honor included twelve "party girls" who were paid $1050 for their contribution to the evening's fun. A bluenose busybody peeked through an open transom just as Fatty and the girls were stripping on the table, decided "decency" had been outraged and called the cops. Attending the festivities were movie magnates Adolph Zukor, Jesse Lasky and Joseph Schenck. They ended up paying $100,000 in hush money to the Boston District Attorney and Mayor James Curley to bury the incident.

It was at another of Fatty's frolics, four years later, that an obscure starlet achieved instant renown. Unfortunately the young lady was in no position to profit from her fame.

Virginia Rappe, a lovely brunette model from Chicago, had attracted some attention when her smiling face appeared under a sunbonnet on the sheet music cover of "Let Me Call You Sweetheart." An offer came from Sennett, and she went to work on his lot, taking minor parts. She also did her share of sleeping around, and gave half the company crabs. This epidemic so shocked Sennett, that he closed down his studio and had it fumigated. Virginia was forgiven, however, and soon started "going steady" with veteran Sennett director

---

← Arbuckle on the witness stand: A frolic turned sour

Henry "Pathé" Lehrman. He gave her a small part in his film Fantasy and later introduced her to Arbuckle when he directed him in Joey Loses a Sweetheart. Virginia's raven-haired beauty was noticed by William Fox when she won a "Best Dressed Girl in Pictures" award; he took her under contract. There was talk of starring Virginia in a Fox feature, Twilight Baby. Virginia Rappe seemed to be on her way.

Arbuckle had his roving eye on Virginia for some time. He had asked her to be leading lady in one of his comedies and had insisted that his friend, Bambina Maude Delmont, bring her to a party celebrating his new three-year $3,000,000 contract with Paramount. Fatty loved liquor and ladies; the more the merrier.

On a whim, Fatty chose San Francisco as the scene of his revel. It would give him the chance to try out his new $25,000 custom-made Pierce-Arrow. On Labor Day weekend two carloads of holidaying film folk roared off in great hilarity on a 450-mile dash up the Coast Highway to the City of

Hills. Fatty and his movie colony cronies, Lowell Sherman and Freddy Fishback, were piled in his flashy Pierce-Arrow, with Virginia Rappe, Bambina Maude Delmont and assorted showgirls in another.

Arriving in the Bay City late Saturday night, Arbuckle checked in at the luxurious Hotel St. Francis, sending the girls on to the Palace. Fatty took three adjoining suites on the 12th floor— enough room for any developments. Fatty rang up his bootleg connection, Tom-Tom the bellboy, found some jazz on the radio, and the party was on.

On Labor Day afternoon, Monday, September 5, 1921, the party was still going strong. It was Fatty's "open house" with people coming and going, the crowd swollen to about fifty and the host a happy drunk. Virginia and the other girls were downing gin-laced Orange Blossoms; some shed their tops to do the shimmy; guests were trading pajama bottoms and the empty bottles were piling up. At about a quarter after three, Arbuckle, flapping around in pajamas and a bathrobe, grabbed Virginia and steered the tipsy model to the bedroom of suite 1221. He gave the revelers his famous leering wink, saying, "This is the chance I've waited for for a long time" and locked the door.

Bambina Maude Delmont later testified that the festivities were stilled when sharp screams rang out in the adjoining bedroom. Weird moans were heard through the door. After much pounding and kicking, a giggling Arbuckle sallied forth in ripped pajamas, Virginia's hat squashed on his head at a crazy angle, and quipped to the girls, "Go in and get her dressed and take her to the Palace. She makes too much noise." When Virginia kept screaming, he yelled, "Shut up or I'll throw you out of the window!"

Bambina and a showgirl friend, Alice Blake, found Virginia nearly nude

on the disordered bed, writhing in pain and moaning, "I'm dying, I'm dying . . . He hurt me." As Alice later testified, "We tried to dress her, but found her clothing torn to shreds. Her shirtwaist, underclothes and even her stockings were ripped and torn so that one could hardly recognize what garments they were."

Virginia was only able to whisper to a nurse in the exclusive Pine Street hospital where she was taken, "Fatty Arbuckle did this to me. Please see that he doesn't get away with it!" before sinking into a coma.

On September 10, one year to the day after the death of Olive Thomas, Virginia Rappe died, age twenty-five, losing forever her chance to star in Twilight Baby.

The cause of her death almost went undiscovered. The San Francisco Deputy Coroner, Michael Brown, suspicious after a "fishy" phone call from the hospital inquiring about a post-mortem, went around personally to see what was going on. What was going on was the beginning of a frantic cover-up. He was just in time to see an orderly emerge from an elevator and head for the hospital's incinerator with a glass jar containing Virginia's injured female organs. He requisitioned the organs from the reluctant doctor so that he could conduct his own examination. Thus it was revealed that Virginia's bladder had been ruptured by some form of violence, which led to her death from peritonitis. Brown reported the matter to his superior, Coroner T.B. Leland, and it was agreed that a police investigation was in order.

Detectives Tom Reagan and Griffith Kennedy were soon grilling the uneasy hospital staff to find out who was covering up what; they found out. So did the newspapers. When Fatty Arbuckle was charged with Virginia Rappe's rape and murder, all the world knew the name of Virginia Rappe. The State of California blamed her death on "external pressure" applied by Arbuckle during sexual dalliance. A forlorn fame for Virginia. A heavy rap for Fatty: "Murder 1."

The shock waves coming from San Francisco that September nearly

Fatty and his Pierce Arrow: The morning after ↑   Suite 1221 at the St. Francis: A heavy rap →

shook Hollywood to its newly laid foundations. It was all too unbelievable: Fatty, kiddies' favorite, Riot o' Laffs Balloonatic, champion of good clean slapstick fun suddenly featured in Movie Star Death Orgy.

ARBUCKLE ORGY RAPER DANCES WHILE VICTIM DIES

As headlines screamed, the rumors flew of a hideously unnatural rape: Arbuckle, enraged at his drunken impotence, had ravaged Virginia with a Coca-Cola bottle, or a champagne bottle, then had repeated the act with a jagged piece of ice . . . or, wasn't it common knowledge that Arbuckle was exceptionally well-endowed? . . . or, was it just a question of 266-pounds-too-much of Fatty flattening Virginia in a flying leap?

What was certain was a leap in

circulation; the tabloids had a field day printing insinuations about Arbuckle's "bottle party." The San Francisco Examiner editorialized: "Hollywood Must Stop Using San Francisco for a Garbage Can." The Coroner was quoted as demanding "steps to prevent a further occurrence of such events, so that San Francisco will not be made the rendezvous of the debauchee and gangster." San Francisco churches demanded retribution for the "sex mad maniac from Hollywood" who chose law-abiding San Francisco for his "shameful revels."

In Hartford, Connecticut, women vigilantes ripped down the screen in a theater showing an Arbuckle comedy, while in Thermopolis, Wyoming, cowhands shot up the screen of a movie house showing an Arbuckle short. Barrages of bottles and eggs were reported. As a "Lynch Fatty" mood swept the land, vigilante groups demanded a clean-up of the whole Hollywood colony; Arbuckle's films were withdrawn.

While Arbuckle sweated it out in a San

Witness Maude Delmont ↑   The tabloid touch: Arbuckle Art ↑

Francisco jail, being held in custody in the grim old Kearny Street Hall of Justice, his lawyers fought to have his first-degree murder charge changed to manslaughter. Adolph Zukor, who had millions at stake on Arbuckle, phoned San Francisco District Attorney Matt Brady in an effort to quash the case. It merely outraged Brady, who later charged he had been offered a bribe. Other prominent movie colony figures called Brady to suggest that Arbuckle shouldn't be crucified just because Virginia Rappe drank too much and died. The D.A. was enraged at these further interventions.

The trial began in mid-November 1921, in San Francisco's Superior Court, with Arbuckle taking the stand to deny any wrongdoing. His attitude seemed to be one of complete indifference to Virginia Rappe; at no point did he express remorse or even sorrow for her death. His lawyers were more out front: a concerted attempt was made to besmirch Virginia's character, suggesting she was "loose" and had slept around in New York, South America and Paris as well as Hollywood. After much conflicting testimony the jury favored acquitting Arbuckle by 10–2 after forty-three hours deliberation. A mistrial was declared.

A second trial jury went 10–2 for conviction and was dismissed. Fatty, who was out on bail, was forced to sell his sedate English home on West Adams Street in L.A. and his fleet of fancy cars to pay lawyers' fees.

Despite the indignant Brady, who wanted to nail Fatty in the worst way, Arbuckle was acquitted in a third trial ending April 12, 1922, largely due to incredibly confused testimony by forty witnesses (mostly drunk at the time of the incident) and the lack of specific evidence (such as a bloody bottle).

The jury that freed Fatty made this comment: "Acquittal is not enough for Roscoe Arbuckle. We feel a grave injustice has been done him and there was not the slightest proof to connect him in any way with the commission of any crime."

On the courtroom steps Arbuckle told the press, "This is the most solemn moment of my life. My innocence of the hideous charge preferred against me has been proved . . . I am truly grateful to my fellow men and women. My life has been devoted to the production of clean pictures

Arbuckle on trial in San Francisco ↑

for the happiness of children. I shall try to enlarge my field of usefulness so that my art shall have a wider service."

His solemn moment of hope was short-lived, however. Fatty was free but not forgiven. Henry Lehrman, Virginia's erstwhile boy friend, had this bitter comment: "Virginia had the most remarkable determination. She would rise from the dead to defend her person from indignity. As for Arbuckle, this is what comes of taking vulgarians from the gutter and giving them enormous salaries and making idols of them. Some people don't know how to get a kick out of life, except in a beastly way. They are the ones who participate in orgies that surpass the orgies of degenerate Rome."

Or, he might have added, Babylon.

Madame Elinor Glyn, the movie colony's tone-setter, took the occasion to comment on Hollywood's rotten apples: "If they are flagrantly immoral, hang them; do not show their pictures; suppress them; but do not make them all suffer for a few. This Arbuckle party was a beastly, disgusting thing and things like it should be stamped out. But I didn't see any such things in Hollywood, and if there are dope parties there, they must be very small."

Paramount cancelled Arbuckle's $3,000,000 contract. His unreleased films were junked, causing the studio a cool million-dollar write-off. Fatty the Funnyman was finished. The Prince of Whales had been harpooned.

Arbuckle was banned from acting. Only a few friends like Buster Keaton remained faithful. It was Keaton who suggested Arbuckle should change his name to "Will B. Good." He did adopt the name of William Goodrich in later years and gained employment as a gag man and comedy director. But Arbuckle wanted to act. He pleaded in the March 1931 Photoplay: "Just let me work. I want to go back to the screen. I think I can entertain and gladden the people that see me. All I want is that. If I do get back, it will be grand. If I don't — well, okay."

Well okay was the way it worked out: Fatty was never allowed to forget his fall from grace. People whistled "I'm Coming, Virginia" when they recognized him in the street. That sticky headline ink wouldn't wash off. The part he was forced to play was Pagliacci.

In his forced retirement Arbuckle took to drinking heavily. Bottles seemed to haunt him. In 1931 Fatty was arrested in Hollywood for drunk driving. As the traffic cop approached, Fatty flung a bottle from the car, laughing, "There goes the evidence!"

Was he thinking of another bottle that went sailing out of the 12th-floor window of the Hotel St. Francis on Labor Day 1921?

Broke and broken, he died at forty-six in New York, June 28, 1933. Poor Fatty! L'affaire Arbuckle scared Hollywood out of ten years growth. Hollywood now meant more than Dreamland. It was forever linked with Scandal in the minds of millions.

Trouble with women ↑

Fatty: Haunted by bottles →

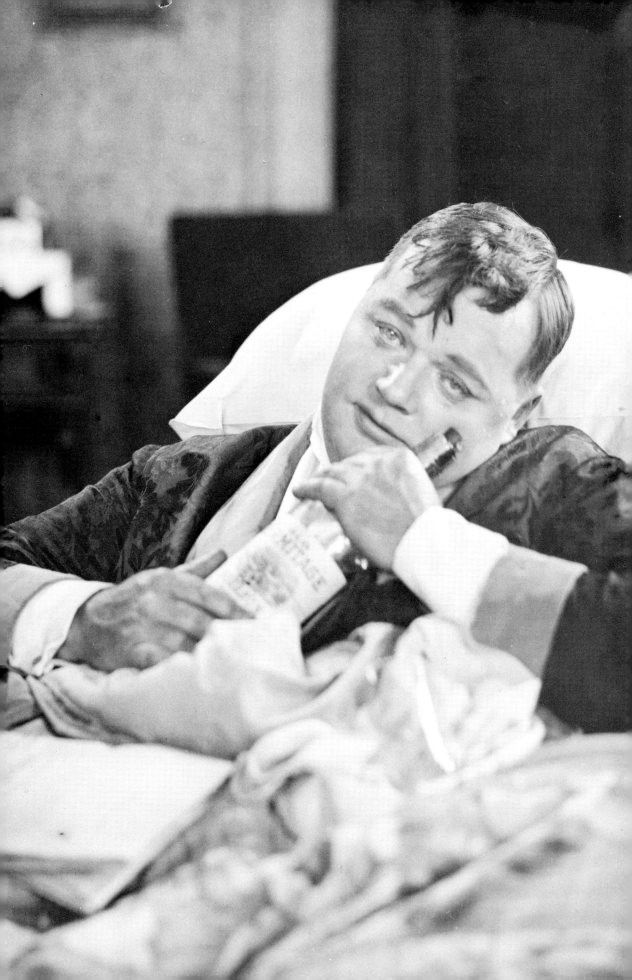

To Miss Hunter —
Mary Hunter
God bless her
from
William Taylor
6/1/20.

·PANIC AT PARAMOUNT·

While Arbuckle sweltered through his second trial in San Francisco and Hollywood simmered in the glare of inflamed public opinion, a scandal broke right in the center of the film colony.

On the night of February 1, 1922, someone killed William Desmond Taylor in the study of his bungalow court apartment on Alvarado Street in L.A.'s placid Westlake district. Taylor was Chief Director of Famous Players-Lasky, a Paramount subsidiary. Paramount, which had its hands full with Arbuckle, could now thank its unlucky stars for another scandal.

The body was discovered the following morning by Taylor's Negro manservant, Henry Peavey. Taylor lay on his back on the floor of the study as if in a trance, his arms straight out, a chair fallen over his legs. Robbery was not the motive; his large "lucky" diamond ring (he had worn it since the success of his first film, The Diamond from the Sky) still shone on his finger.

Peavey ran, emitting a soprano scream, "Dey've kilt Massa! Dey've kilt Massa!" (as reported in the Los Angeles Examiner) waking up the other residents of the court, including Edna Purviance, who immediately placed a phone call to Mabel Normand. Mabel called

Charles Eyton, general manager of Famous Players-Lasky who, in turn, called the Paramount super-chief, Adolph Zukor. Edna placed another call to Paramount star Mary Miles Minter. She could not be reached. The message was left with her mother, Mrs. Charlotte Shelby. None of these saw fit to notify the police. They all had urgent business to attend to first.

Mabel rushed to Taylor's to retrieve a bundle of her correspondence. Charles Eyton rushed to Taylor's to get rid of all the illegal liquor. (Dead or alive, a Paramount director must not be found violating the Eighteenth Amendment!) Adolph Zukor rushed to Taylor's to clean up any signs of sexual hanky-panky. Charlotte Shelby rushed to her daughter Mary with the news, which precipitated an unseemly match of shouted hysterics. Henry Peavey, the soprano manservant, traipsed up and down sedate Alvarado Street like a demented thing, incessantly screaming, "Dey've kilt Massa! Dey've kilt Massa!" until, much later, some neighbor phoned the cops to "come collect the crazy coon." Representatives of the law did eventually arrive.

When the police arrived at Taylor's bungalow later that morning

← William Desmond Taylor: Dead center

a busy scene was underway. Merry flames blazed in the fireplace, fed compromising papers by Paramount's top brass, while Edna Purviance looked on. Mabel Normand, the Sennett heroine, was poking into nooks and crannies for the misplaced correspondence. The still eye of the hurricane was Taylor's corpse on the study floor, two .38 bullets in his heart.

There might have been some hope of solving the enigma if the Paramount bigwigs had not swooped down on the dead man's house to cosmeticize the scene. It is more than likely that significant clues were incinerated by Zukor and Eyton in Taylor's fireplace.

Zukor, Eyton & Co. did not, however, have time to complete their housecleaning. When the homicide squad descended on the Taylor bungalow, all kinds of things came to light. The cops uncovered a cache of pornographic photographs hidden behind some scenarios at the bottom of a drawer. These whimsical

portraits of the dead man in the identifiable company of several female stars confirmed his reputation as a Lothario, if not his tact. Several prominent actresses were questioned, including Mary Pickford, whose large framed photograph inscribed to Taylor was found. The photographic curiosities contributed nothing to solve the case; Mary Pickford said she would "pray."

When Mabel Normand was questioned about her early-morning browse, she candidly admitted that she had been looking for letters she had written to Taylor, to prevent them being examined by outsiders. She commented, "I admit this, but it was only for one purpose, to prevent terms of affection from being misconstrued." (The letters were later found tucked into one of Taylor's riding boots.)

Further sleuthing in the Taylor study shook loose a letter hidden between the pages of White Stains, a book of erotica by Aleister Crowley. When the scented page fluttered to the floor it was seen not to have been penned by Mabel

← Mabel as The Slim Princess   ↑ Lothario Taylor   Mary Miles Minter: Demure innocence? ↑

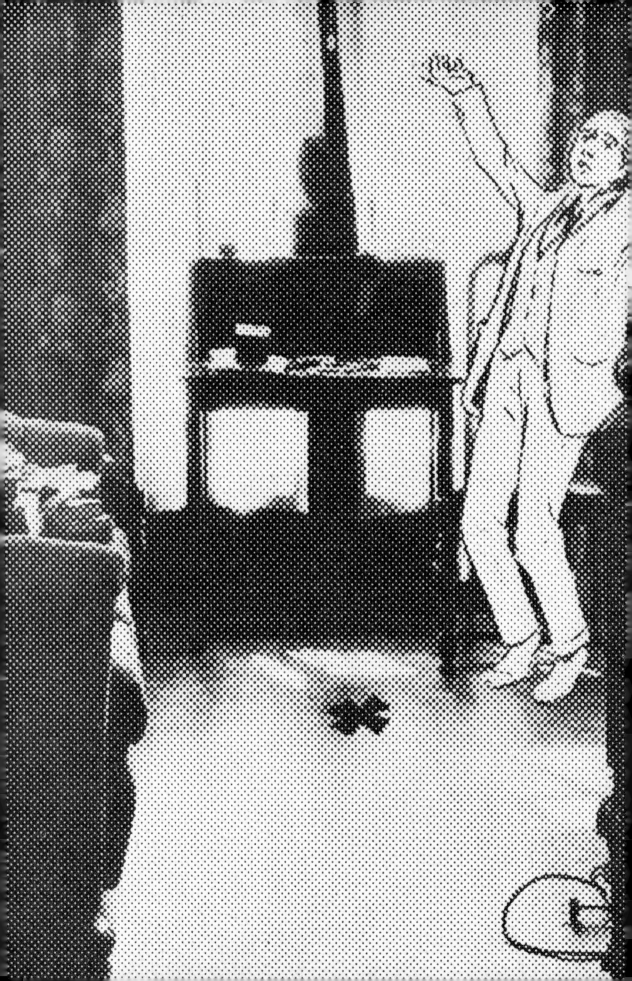

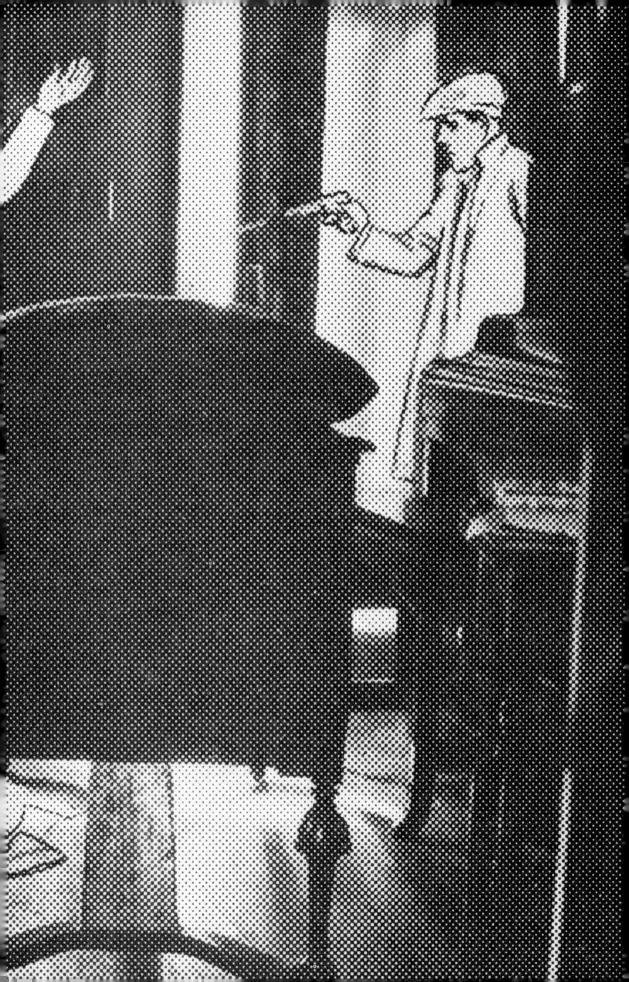

Normand. The pale pink stationery was monogrammed M.M.M. and eyebrows were immediately raised. Mary Miles Minter was Paramount's answer to Mary Pickford, curls and all, an embodiment of demure innocence. Yet here in her handwriting was a mash note which ran:

Dearest—
I love you — I love you — I love you —
X X X X X X X X X X X X X X X X X X X
Yours always!
Mary

When questioned, Mary confirmed her ardor: "I did love William Desmond Taylor. I loved him deeply and tenderly, with all the admiration a young girl gives to a man with the poise and position of Mr. Taylor." (M.M.M. was twenty-two; Taylor fifty.)

At the garish, crowded funeral a distraught Mary Miles Minter approached the bier and kissed Taylor's

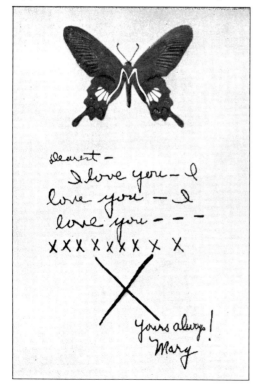

corpse full on the lips. She then caused a considerable stir by rising to announce that the corpse had spoken! "He whispered something to me; it sounded like 'I shall love you always, Mary!'"

The circumstances of the Taylor murder were so bizarre that they have been incorporated into several mystery novels and movie scenarios. And all the real-life cast were "characters" — even Taylor's soprano manservant, Peavey, who liked to crochet doilies and scarves. Then there was Taylor's butler, Sands. He was missing. It turned out he was the director's younger brother — a dubious figure with a larcenous past, on the lam from the law. Taylor had coached him to acquire an impeccably servile demeanor, his disguise further enhanced by bleached hair. Sands, suspected for passing forged checks and possible involvement in his brother's death, had vanished, never to be seen again.

It turned out that both Mary Miles Minter and Mabel Normand had paid Taylor a visit the night of the crime. Mabel was the last person to see him alive. As a parting gift, the ever-thoughtful Taylor had given Mabel the latest volume of Freud.

Ten minutes after the departure of Mabel's limousine, a neighbor, Mrs. Faith Cole MacLean, heard a loud noise and went to the window overlooking Taylor's bungalow. Later she told police: "I wasn't sure, then, that it was a shot at all, but I distinctly heard an explosion. Then I glanced out of my window and I saw a man leaving the house and going down the walk. I suppose it was a man. It was dressed like a man, but you know, funny-looking. It was dressed in a heavy coat with a muffler around the chin and a cap pulled down over the eyes. But it walked like a woman —

← X marks the spot ↑

quick little steps and broad hips and short legs." (Could this have been Mary Miles Minter's jealous mother, Mrs. Shelby, in drag? She owned a .38 caliber pearl-handled revolver, and had been seen practicing shooting it shortly before the murder. Afterwards, she was allowed to slip away to Europe without questioning.) It was an enigma that would even have baffled S. S. Van Dine.

The murder threw Hollywood into an uproar. The incident was particularly shattering to the film colony since Taylor, a social figure of prominence, had been president of the Screen Directors' Guild. A handsome, worldly fellow, bibliophile and supposed bachelor with a reputation as a ladies' man, he was in reality William Deane-Tanner, who had vanished from his New York home in 1908, leaving a wife and daughter.

It soon came out that in his Hollywood incarnation he had been carrying on simultaneous affairs with Mabel Normand, Mary Miles Minter and Charlotte Shelby, Mary's mother. This "quadrangle" held all that the tabloids could desire in the way of sensation. The papers also insinuated that Taylor had been the cause of the suicide of Zelda Crosby, a Famous Players screenwriter with whom he had been intimate.

While ransacking Taylor's bungalow the inspectors came upon a more esoteric aspect of the director's dalliances. In a locked closet of his bedroom was found a unique collection of Hollywood lingerie—lacy, deluxe ladies' undies, each tagged with initials and a date. (It seems that "lucky dog" Desmond made a point of retaining a souvenir of each sentimental encounter.) When a pale pink nightgown of filmy silk, delicately embroidered M.M.M., was found, Mary Miles Minter's sweet virginal image was ruined and her career smashed. (In forced retirement, M.M.M. turned to the consolation of comfort-eating and rapidly put on weight.) The Drums of Fate was her last picture.

As if all this did not suffice, there was a "dope angle" to the case. Reporters stated that Taylor had recently been visiting the "queer meeting places" in L.A. and Hollywood, dens where strange effeminate men and peculiarly masculine women dressed in kimonos

Taylor as director: A shattering incident ↑

39

sat in circles, where guests were served marijuana, opium and morphine, the drugs wheeled in on tea carts. It was soon revealed that Taylor's good friend Mabel Normand, whose antic clowning for Sennett gained her fans by the millions, owed her effervescence at least in part to Cocaine & Co. Mabel's monthly expenditure for "cokey" was in the neighborhood of $2000, blackmail included.

On one occasion Taylor had confronted a blackmailer who was hounding Miss Normand, and in the ensuing sidewalk fisticuffs knocked him flat.

When she became involved in the "dope angle" of the Taylor case, it was Normand's turn to retire from the screen. Suzanna, the Sennett feature she had just completed, was withdrawn after it had been boycotted. The epitaph to her career was an editorial in Good Housekeeping,

suggesting Mabel was too "adulterated" for family consumption. The delightful comedienne of so many Keystone Comedies was no longer an apple in the eye of her former fans.

Though Mabel Normand and Mary Miles Minter stood out as the principal scapegoats in the Taylor case, all of Hollywood felt the heat. Howls went up around the country at this new proof of filmland depravity. 1922 was a rough year for the movie industry.

Stacks of uncomplimentary press notices continued to pour in; denunciations rang out from the pulpits. It was not divine wrath the magnates feared, but retaliation at the box office. The specter of collective boycott by women's clubs, church organizations and anti-vice committees seemed formidable. With the professional puritans clamoring for a clean-up, something had to be done to improve the movies' image — fast.

Mrs. Shelby and daughter Mary going to fat ↑　　　　**Mary Miles Minter: Guilt by association →**

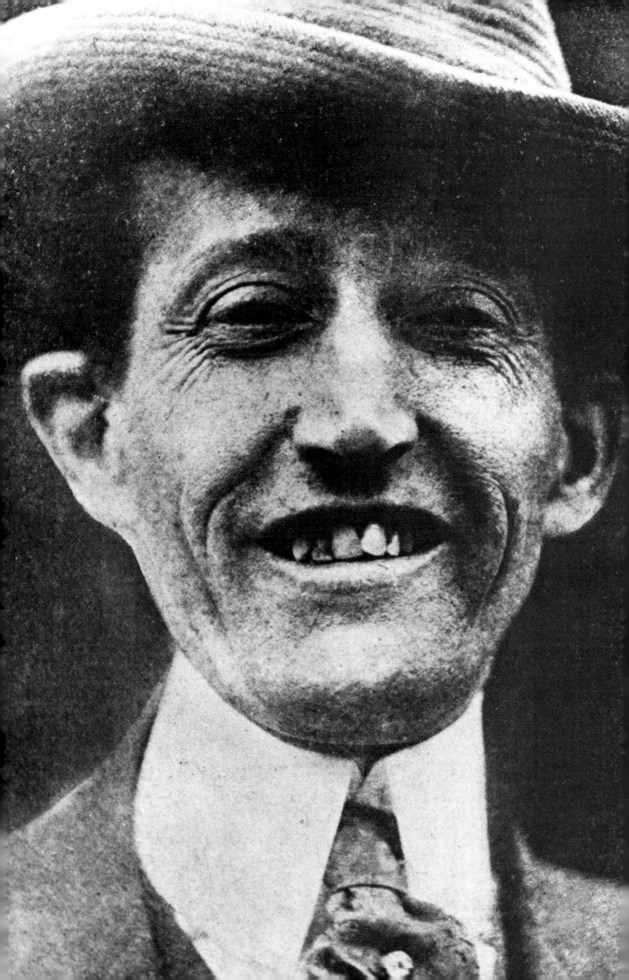

· HAYS FEVER ·

The "improvement" of the movies' image entailed a bit of window dressing borrowed from the world of baseball. The multimillion-dollar sports business had nearly been scuttled in 1919 when a World Series "fix" came to light. The baseball bosses found a $50,000 solution to their predicament by making Judge Kenesaw Mountain Landis their keep-the-game-clean-boys czar. The Hollywood bosses decided a similar figurehead of moral rectitude was badly needed to umpire movie morals. They doubled the ante.

The plush $100,000-a-year job of Movie Czar was offered to a prim-faced, bat-eared, mealy-mouthed political chiseler: Will H. Hays, a member of President Harding's unfortunate Cabinet, who as chairman of the Republican National Committee had tilted the nomination to Harding. (In 1928 it came out that supposed simon-pure Hays had accepted a $75,000 "gift" and a $185,000 "loan" from oilman Harry "Teapot Dome" Sinclair, in gratitude for pushing easygoing Harding into the White House. The devious Hays told a Senate committee three different stories about these bribes; Senator Borah alleged that "Hays caused the Republican Party to sell itself to the willful despoilers of the nation." Hays barely wriggled out of that one;

in 1930 he was caught red-handed paying expense money, honoraria and salaries to "moral" leaders who were supposed to render impartial opinions on the purity of films for various religious and civic organizations. Shifty Hays got away with it.)

As Harding's Postmaster General, Hays opposed smut in the mails. Thus this Hoosier Presbyterian elder, who was also a member of the Masons, Knights of Pythias, Kiwanians, Rotarians, Moose and Elks, seemed just right to give the purity leagues satisfaction. Harding accepted the resignation of his sly postal watchdog and Hays left for his office in New York — a city considered "neutral" territory, far from the fleshpots of Hollywood but close to the powerful film financiers.

In March 1922, Hays became Czar of the Movies: president of the hastily-formed Motion Picture Producers and Distributors of America, Inc. In the company of a rather uptight gathering of founding fathers — Adolph Zukor, Marcus Loew, Carl Laemmle, William Fox, Samuel Goldwyn, Lewis and Myron Selznick — a press conference was called to let the world know what Hollywood's new look would be. (Elinor Glyn cynically predicted, "Whatever will bring in the most money will happen.")

← Shifty Hays   Hays signs up with founding fathers of filmland →

From the Kansas City Star, February 20, 1922.

The rookie policeman of movie morals waded right in with a barrage of hogwash: "The potentialities of motion pictures for moral influence and education are limitless. Therefore its integrity should be protected as we protect the integrity of our children and our schools, and its quality developed as we develop the quality of our schools . . . Above all is our duty to youth. We must have toward that sacred thing, the mind of a child, toward that clean and virgin thing, that unmarked slate — we must have toward that the same responsibility, the same care about the impression made upon it, that the best teacher or the best clergyman, the most inspired teacher of youth, would have." As Hays intoned, the founding fathers of filmland broke out in shit-eating grins and heads bobbed agreement for the cameras. Politics had taught Hays all he needed to know about hypocrisy.

The Hays Office issued its first diktat: films were to be purified. Screen immorality would be scissored: no more improprieties; no more lingering, lusty kisses; no more carnality; the axe for off-screen cut-ups. The picture people were about to observe a perpetual Lent. Morals clauses would be inserted into all contracts to persuade the Golden People to shape up: male stars would henceforth be monks and women stars nuns. Capers would be punished by the boot.

Hays fever swept the front offices. The moguls had no illusions that the morals clause would get the colony to mend its ways. They launched an undercover investigation of everybody in sight and turned loose a frantic, competing horde of private eyes on Hollywood. Detectives used the whole bag of dirty tricks from bribing servants to peering in windows, even primitive "listening devices." When the reports came in, the front offices died a little. It was much, much worse than they had suspected. With the approval of Czar Hays, a Doom Book was compiled with a total of 117 Hollywood names deemed "unsafe" because of their no longer private lives.

· GOOD TIME WALLY ·

When the Doom Book was shown to Adolph Zukor, the head of Paramount Pictures had cause for alarm. Leading the blacklist was the name of his top box-office draw, Wallace Reid. Zukor, whose studio had already sustained a staggering loss when public outcry forced withdrawal of all Arbuckle and Mary Miles Minter pictures, bitterly protested the proposed banning of his popular star: "You should know that you are asking the impossible. Why, it would mean a two-million-dollar loss to us to do a thing like this in the case of this one man — a thing like this would simply be suicide." The other studio chiefs behind the blacklist knew there were ways to force the hand even of powerful Zukor, and leaked the inside dope on Reid to the ever-avid tabloids. The GraphiC led off with the banner headline:

HOLLYWOOD HOP-HEADS

insinuating that among prominent film colony drug addicts was a certain very popular male star at Paramount. These rumors were suddenly confirmed in a startling manner when Wally Reid, the "King of Paramount," was spirited away to a secluded private sanitarium in March 1922.

The commitment papers had been signed by Florence, Reid's unhappy wife, a featured player at Universal under the name of Dorothy Davenport. Papa Laemmle, among others, had counseled Florence that Wally's "cure" was a pressing matter. She heartily agreed, and even Zukor reluctantly concurred it was better that Wally be kept out of sight.

Paramount issued some euphemisms about Reid's "overwork" but soon Mrs. Wallace Reid herself informed the press that her husband was undergoing a cure for morphine addiction.

The sensational news that Wally Reid was a drug addict stunned the American public. Wally was not just a popular movie star, he was the vital exponent of Young American Manhood. Blue-eyed, chestnut-haired Wally was a cheerful, strapping six-foot-three giant, possessed of great charm and acting ability as well as youth and good looks. Now, his nickname, "Good Time Wally," took on another meaning.

In his new role as Hollywood image doctor, Will Hays tried to cushion the shock by announcing that "the unfortunate Mr. Reid should be dealt with as a diseased person — not be censured, shunned."

Wally Reid was indeed dealt with as a diseased person, and one best

---

← Airing his basket: Rugged Wally Reid   Wally's "Den of Iniquity": Cocaine in the trophy cup →

kept out of sight. He spent the remainder of 1922 within a padded cell of that private sanitarium. The abrupt withdrawal of his daily morphine fix and the shock of abrupt confinement unhinged his mind. Wally became obsessed with the idea that he had been railroaded — he was right.

Paramount had pushed him through a nonstop production schedule of "Wallace Reid Racing Features" —

All in the Family: Dorothy, Wally and kids ↑   Mary Miles Minter moons for her hero: Wally Reid →

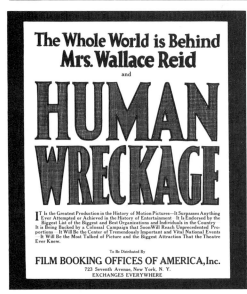
The Roaring Road, What's Your Hurry?, Double Speed — that had little to recommend them but the personality of the star behind the wheel. The gruelling pace began to tell, and in 1920, while he was working on Forever, at the prompting from a quiet, gentlemanly actor from the Sennett lot, Wally took his first morphine fix to mask his exhaustion and bolster his energy. By the time the film was in the can, Wally was hooked. Toward the end, working on Clarence, they actually propped Wally before the camera in order to finish the picture.

Wally died in his padded cell on January 18, 1923, age thirty. A rumor swept the movie colony that he had been "put to sleep."

At the time of Wally's death, his wife, Florence, hastened to call a press conference. She announced her intention to avenge her husband's death. She had turned over to the police the names of Wally's friends who had (according to her) drawn him into a life of drink, dope and debauchery. They called themselves the "Hollywood Hell-Raisers," but she preferred to qualify them as "Bohemians." "Gradually, he got to drinking with his Bohemian friends, and soon this wasn't a home. It was a roadhouse. Wally's friends would come in here by the scores, at any odd hour of the day or night. They came, they stayed, they drank. It was one wild party after another, each one worse than the last. Nobody could do anything with Wally. And then — morphine."

Florence also took the opportunity to announce that her next picture would be Human Wreckage, an exposé of dope traffic. She was doing this film to "warn the nation's youth" as well as "in memory of Wally." She did not mention she had covert assistance from Will Hays for this antiseptic film. She concluded her interview with a final comment on her dead husband: "Wally was cured, but terribly debilitated physically. Only a return to the drug under control could have saved him. He refused."

On her subsequent cross-country lecture tour to warn of the dangers of drug addiction and launch Human Wreckage, her opportunistic billing was always "Mrs. Wallace Reid."

Mary Pickford provided Wally with a professional epitaph: "His death is a very great tragedy. I know he would have lived down every mistake he made."

WALLY REID-HIS CHAIR
HIS FRIENDS ARE WELCOME
WHEN HE IS NOT ON THE SET

Professional widow, Mrs. Wallace Reid, leaves on tour →

· CHAMPAGNE BATHS ·

Will Hays issued a front-line communiqué promising better days for 1923: "We are traveling the highway to better things in filmdom . . . soon there will be a model Hollywood . . . I have faith that unfortunate incidents will be things safely of the past . . ."

These pious pronouncements did not tone down the exhibitors' blurbs: Such films as Woman to Woman, Men and The Bedroom Window promised a peek at "beautiful jazz babies, champagne baths, midnight revels, petting parties in the purple dawn" as well as "neckers . . . white kisses . . . red kisses . . . pleasure mad daughters, sensation-craving mothers . . . the Truth — Bold, Naked, Sensational!" Forty million Americans paid tribute every week at the box office, urged by ads that "All the adventure, all the romance, all the excitement you lack in your daily life are in — Pictures! They take you completely out of yourself into a wonderful new world — Out of the cage of everyday existence! If only for an afternoon or an evening — Escape!" The masses of the Twenties thought it was a "swell" idea, even when Hays tacked a moral message on the end.

The rule of Czar Hays was looked at with dismay by Hollywood's sincere believers in film artistry, who saw the advent of the big scissors man from the Bible Belt as an unmitigated catastrophe for the Seventh Muse. "Photoplays which deal honestly with life are now banned from the screen," they pointed out, "while claptrap receives a benediction provided it has a blantantly moral ending and serves up its sex appeal with hypocritical disapproval." (They were aiming at that bathroom turncoat, Cecil B. De Mille.) Hays' concern for "the mind of a child . . . that unmarked slate" meant in practice that screen content was often reduced to the level of a ten-year-old. A disgruntled Hollywood wag made up a photo-montage showing Hays as a happy baby in a sand pile; it was much circulated at parties he did not attend.

Although public behavior was somewhat toned down, the movie colony's parties were as rowdy as before. Hotel suites were carefully avoided as unsuitable locations for high jinks. The Golden People had their incredible brand-new Hispano-Mauresque villas for private playpens — and they were careful to draw the brocaded drapes and to post guards at the wrought-iron gates to bar studio snoops and reporters. Then the darlings of the

The Flapper

equipment is not always equal to the strain. They have money, an unaccustomed toy, and they spend it in bizarre ways. They may indulge in 'wild parties' or they may indulge in other forms of relaxation and excitement. Many of them spend all they make . . . Since Prohibition came in many of them who had no liquor stocks turned to other stimulants. The dealers in illicit drugs find a growing market in Hollywood."

While the Journal was correct in its comments on the drug traffic, it was wrong in assuming the film folk had any difficulty finding intoxicating beverages. Each star had his or her own 'legger, and rumrunning to the Hollywood haciendas was a lucrative business.

gods could cut loose.

Rumors of riotous Hollywood high life behind Hays' back seeped out to the press through bribed butlers and upstairs maids, and the New York Journal commented: "When people spring from poverty to affluence within a few weeks, their mental

The movie colony slaked its thirst with a vengeance during Prohibition but much of the illicit alcohol was of questionable quality. Art Accord, the horse-opera star, was driven to suicide by bad-booze insanity; western star Leo Maloney was killed by it.

Flapper Joan Crawford Charlestons in Our Dancing Daughters →

*Lest you forget
Barbara
La
Marr*

· HEROIN HEROINES ·

After the death of Wally Reid, Hollywood "users" did not break their habits, they learned discretion. One of the town's leading dealers was a quiet, gentlemanly actor on the Sennett lot known as "The Count." It was he who offered to fix up Wally Reid's hangover during the filming of Forever, who first put Mabel Normand, Juanita Hansen, Barbara La Marr and Alma Rubens on the junk.

"The Girl Who Is Too Beautiful," Barbara La Marr, was Hollywood's most glamorous, if jaded, junkie. She dabbled in every known variety of dope until her fatal OD at twenty-six, in 1926. Barbara kept her cocaine in a golden casket on the grand piano; her opium was the finest grade Benares blend. Barbara, the Southern belle brought into films by Douglas Fairbanks in The Three Musketeers, seemed to know she was not long for this life. Determined to make the most of it, she boasted of never wasting any more than two hours on sleep a night — she had "better things to do." She did, indeed, have lovers by the dozens — "like roses" she said — as well as six husbands during her brief career as a star.

The film titles of "Too Beautiful" Barbara read like a litany: Souls for Sale, Strangers of the Night, The White Moth. Her last incarnation as a femme fatale was in The Heart of a Siren. Her own heart was stopped soon after by a suicidal OD. The studio blamed her death on "too rigorous dieting."

After Barbara La Marr, the sensitive dramatic actress Alma Rubens lost her "secure foothold on the ladder of fame" to plunge into the night-land of narcotics. The raven-haired star of The Half Breed, The Firefly of Tough Luck, The Price She Paid and Show Boat became a real-life heroin heroine with most of her energies and a great part of her fortune devoted to securing drugs.

Alma's addiction did not become public knowledge until a bizarre incident occurred the afternoon of January 26, 1929 on Hollywood Boulevard. She was to be seen running down the street pursued by two men. "I'm being kidnapped! I'm being kidnapped!" she screamed, tearing off her hat and gloves as she sprinted and throwing them into the gutter with her purse.

She ran up to a gas station and sought refuge among the pumps. The two men caught up with her. Alma then struck savagely with a knife she had concealed in her dress, stabbing the younger of the two men in the

---

← Barbara La Marr: Too Much

shoulder. The gas station attendant managed to grab the knife while the older man locked her arms behind her. Alma, sobbing, was led off to an ambulance parked in front of her house on Wilton Place.

When the story appeared in the papers it became known that Alma Rubens had stabbed the ambulance attendant and that the older man was her physician, Dr. E.W. Meyer. Alma had panicked when they arrived at her house to put her in a private sanitarium. After a few weeks of treatment at the Alhambra Clinic she was allowed to return home with a nurse to look after her. In April 1929 she lashed out at the nurse with a knife and was subdued after a tussle. Alma was taken to the psycho ward of L.A. General Hospital, then transferred to the California State Hospital for the Insane at Patton for a six month "cure." When she left the hospital Alma declared, "I am feeling wonderful again after my rest. I am going to New York and try to pick up my career again, first on stage. Then I hope to return to Hollywood."

Alma's hopes for a Broadway

comeback did not work out, and while in New York she filed divorce proceedings against her third husband, leading man Ricardo Cortez. Alma kept her word and did return to Hollywood in 1931, but soon after her arrival felt a prompting to visit Agua Caliente, across the Mexican border, driving down in the company of Ruth Palmer, a young actress she had brought from New York.

On her return trip to Hollywood they stopped off at the U.S. Grant Hotel in San Diego, where Alma was arrested on January 6, 1931, charged with possession of forty cubes of morphine. The tip-off had come from Ruth Palmer, alarmed at Alma's outbursts of violence. The police found the drug cubes sewn into the seams of one of Alma's dresses when they searched the hotel room. When the cops entered, Alma screamed: "I've been robbed of $9,000 in jewels and this is a frame-up! I came back to California to make a comeback . . . then this has to happen to me!"

After being charged, Alma was diagnosed as seriously ill. She was

Sincerely
Alma Rubens

← Alma Rubens: Many dramas   Barbara La Marr ↑   Alma Rubens, shortly before her death →

The Two-Fold Purpose of
THE JUANITA HANSEN
FOUNDATION

Juanita Hansen
Modern Crusader

My Creed . . .

All great beauty in books, in music, in paint or marble or
clay . . . all great service of whatever kind . . . have been
inspired by men and women with definite goals . . . I, too,
have a definite goal: to help the thousands of narcotic addicts
now living in darkness—alone, ashamed, bewildered. And to
do all I can, to enlist the help of as many others as I can, in
a crusade against the spread of this most dreadful of spiritual
and physical diseases—narcotic addiction.

— *Juanita Hansen.*

their way out." On January 22, 1931, Alma died, age thirty-three.

Another heroin heroine was the delicate blonde Juanita Hansen, "The Original Mack Sennett Girl," who was introduced to drugs on the Keystone lot. "The Count" had approached Juanita early one Monday morning when she was suffering the effects of a boozed-up weekend. He used his usual opener: "Hangover, honey? I'll fix it for you." The first "taste" was free. The die was cast.

Soon, Juanita was buying at $75 an ounce. Years later, she recalled meeting her connection in downtown L.A. at Fourth and Spring Street: ". . . a peddler, the same man who had met me that fateful day at the same spot and had sold me my first 'bundle' of heroin. I had been his best customer since. The man was really a fairly well-known actor, though not a star. I took a dose right there. Doctors, the hospital and the dangers I was running from, meant nothing to me. All I craved was heroin. I bought a good supply." And so "The Count" led another star down Smack Alley.

While Barbara La Marr and Alma Rubens somehow escaped the Doom Book blacklist following the death of Wally Reid, Juanita Hansen was not so fortunate. Her name was found in a letter of an Oakland doctor with whom she had sought treatment, and soon after Reid's death she was arrested and held in jail for seventy-two hours to determine if she was on the stuff. At that time she was not, but the headlines finished her career. Juanita, the daredevil serial queen and star of The Lost City, hit the oblivion trail. Her comeback was not in the movies, but as founder of the Juanita Hansen Foundation, whose avowed aim was to urge doctors to wage war against addiction "as they now crusade against syphilis."

allowed to return home with her mother, under constant medical care. Realizing she was dying, Alma called the Los Angeles Examiner for a last interview: "I have been miserable for so long. I only went to professional men to seek relief from my pain. Each time they said, 'Take this for the pain and you will be able to go on.' When they first started giving me this horrible poison I did not know what it was. I went from one to the other. One even laughed when I told him I craved the drug and said, 'Don't be afraid, you will not need any more after you are well!' But they went on and on giving me this thing. As long as my money held out I could get drugs. I was afraid to tell my mother, my best friends. My only desire has been to get drugs and take them in secrecy. If only I could go on my knees before the police or before a judge and beg them to make stiffer laws so that men will refuse to take dirty dollars from murderers who sell this poison and who escape punishment when caught by buying

Juanita Hansen's comeback ↑

"Too Beautiful" Barbara →

BARBARA LA MARR
WITH GOD IN THE JOY AND BEAUTY OF YOUTH
1896   1926

· THE NEW GODS ·

Despite the morals clause added to their contracts, the admonitions from Hays and the men in the front offices and the glaring examples of fallen stars, the revel in the charmed circle went on unabated through the Roaring Twenties.

The New Gods were determined to live their own legends to the hilt — and to hell with Hays and the Mrs. Grundys of America. The excesses of the stars developed a cynicism and defiance characteristic of Jazz Age youth. Bitterness and darkness often lay just beyond, but their attitude seemed to be "So What!" Edna St. Vincent Millay provided a succinct guide for the Golden People:

My candle burns at both ends;
It will not last the night;
But ah, my foes, and oh, my friends —
It gives a lovely light!

"Oh, the parties we used to have!" La Swanson later recalled. "In those days the public wanted us to live like kings and queens. So we did — and why not? We were in love with life. We were making more money than we ever dreamed existed and there was no reason to believe it would ever stop."

While their foes fulminated, the Hollywood in-crowd whooped it up in an atmosphere of staggering luxury: Spanish–Moorish dream castles like Valentino's hilltop Falcon Lair, with its black marble, black leather bedroom; Marion Davies' hundred-room Ocean House at Santa Monica with its all-gold salon, two bars, private movie theater, old masters and huge marble bridge-spanned swimming pool; Pola Negri's Roman plunge in her living room and Barbara La Marr's enormous sunken bath with its gold fixtures in her all-onyx bathroom; Harold Lloyd's Greenacres, a forty-room fortress with fountains to rival Tivoli; Gloria Swanson's golden bathtub in her black marble bathroom; Tom Mix's rainbow-colored fountain in his dining room; John Gilbert's schooner, The Temptress, his motorboat, The Vampire, his sailboat, The Harpie, his dingy, The Witch and his Cossack servants and private balalaika orchestra; Clara Bow's Chinese den and Charles Ray's solid-gold doorknobs.

If Wally Reid's robin's egg blue McFarlan was no longer seen cruising down Sunset, there was enough gaudy horsepower to take its place: Clara Bow in her red Kissel convertible with chow dogs to match; Valentino's custom-built Voisin tourer with its coiled-cobra

radiator cap; Mae Murray's canary yellow Pierce-Arrow or more formal white Rolls-Royce with liveried chauffeur and ever-present Borzoi; Olga Petrova's purple Packard touring sedan; Gloria Swanson's leopard-upholstered Lancia.

It was a time when Joseph Urban boudoirs were soaked in Shalimar, when $3000 Parisian beaded gowns lasted the life of one party, when sex came served in Arabian

← Harold Lloyd's Chinese den

Mae Murray's Royal Wedding →

Nights splendor, when money came in by the bushel and went out by the fistful, when liquor was clandestine but plentiful and any star could buy the key to an artificial paradise.

The stars worked hard all week, bedtime was usually at ten to be ready for early morning calls; weekends were wild, however. As if dressing up under the klieg lights all week long wasn't enough, a favorite divertissement was the costume party.

Characteristic was Marion Davies' 1926 costume ball held in the Ambassador ballroom, which had been transformed into a lavish Hawaiian scene for the occasion. Mary Pickford came as Lillian Gish in La Bohème; Douglas Fairbanks was Don Q, Son of Zorro; Charlie Chaplin was Napoleon; Jack Gilbert came as Red Grange in football togs and red wig; Lillian Gish was one of Jane Austen's heroines; Bebe Daniels

came as a silver-lamé Joan of Arc; Madame Elinor Glyn was Catherine of Russia; Marshall Neilan and Allan Dwan came disguised as the bearded Smith Brothers of cough-drop fame; while Miss Davies herself appeared in the costume of a nineteenth-century belle. (John Barrymore was such a realistic tramp he was almost refused admission.)

The stars were also costumed in the height of fashion for any appearance in public, with La Swanson leading the parade down Peacock Alley. Gloria's yearly clothes bill itemized at: fur coats, $25,000; other wraps, $10,000; gowns, $50,000; stockings, $9000; shoes, $5000; lingerie, $10,000; purses, $5000; headdresses, $5000 and a $6000 cloud of perfume. At the time, Gloria was collecting $900,000 a year from Paramount. Changing husbands five times was also part of Gloria's showmanship; sic transit Gloria mundi.

La Swanson's shoes, jewels, gowns: Expensive tastes

· CHARLIE'S NYMPHS ·

While Hollywood's naively exhibitionistic Golden People romped through the Roaring Twenties at a killing pace, there existed in their midst a slight, solitary figure dedicated to the Film as Art. This man was British, and British he would remain.

Charles Spencer Chaplin attended other people's parties — the fancy-dress, not the "wild" kind — but he was never known to throw one. This perfectionist preferred to build his own studio on land he purchased on the corner of Sunset Boulevard and La Brea, and spent months on costly retakes on his pictures. Chaplin did not seek out scandal, scandal came to him.

Chaplin had been the subject of diverse speculations in the film colony since his meteoric rise to fame. Some of these speculations dealt with his alleged avariciousness, but the most popular theme for gossip was the way the little man had with women. His name was linked at various times with Edna Purviance, Lila Lee, Josephine Dunn, Anna Q. Nilson, Thelma Morgan Converse, May Collins, Claire Windsor, Clare Sheridan and Pola Negri.

A "big" woman in Charlie's love life was also one of the world's richest: the original gold-digging Ziegfeld girl, Peggy Hopkins Joyce. She cruised into Hollywood with a three-million-dollar bankroll (alimony from five husbands) in the scandal-streaked year of 1922, just to see if the most talked-about "sin city" in the world measured up to its reputation.

Peggy arrived in Hollywood dressed in chic-est black, set off by a display of emeralds and diamonds; a young man had just taken his life on her account in Paris. Her mourning was confined to her wardrobe, however, and soon she and Chaplin were having dîner à deux. Her opener had a certain showgirl candor: "Is it true what all the girls say—that you're hung like a horse?"

The big blonde and the "Little Fellow" were soon enjoying a summer sojourn on the island of Catalina, Charlie having set aside preparations for his next project, Napoleon, to indulge this idyll.

Charlie and Peggy sought out a secluded cove on the far side of the island where they could picnic and do some nude bathing, unobserved — or so they believed. The presence of the two celebrities on the little island had not gone unnoticed, however, and several of the more intrepid native Catalinans had

---

← Chaplin squires two beauties: Gloria Swanson and Marion Davies

CATALINA

LOVELY ISLE OF THE SEA

COMPLIMENTS OF
Catalina Island Museum Soc
CASINO BLDG
Avalon, California

Lyric by
Elizabeth
Renton

Music by
George
Rozier

25¢
NET

E·B·RENTON
PUBLISHER

AVALON.   CATALINA ISLAND
CALIF.

hiked up the mountain overlooking the cove, equipped with powerful binoculars. Soon afterwards the wild goats native to Catalina acquired the nickname "Charlies."

During their brief but intense friendship, Peggy regaled Chaplin with the story of her life as a gold-digging adventuress. Chaplin put these anecdotes to good use, several incidents in Peggy's early career providing him with the necessary inspiration for his film A Woman of Paris.

The "little" women in Charlie's Hollywood career established his reputation as a chicken hawk. The first nymphet was blonde little Mildred Harris, who was fourteen when she and Charlie met at a blanket party on Santa Monica beach. She was just sixteen when Charlie asked her to marry him. He had been informed of her pregnancy

and it seemed the sporting thing to do.

Their marriage on October 23, 1918 was but forty-eight hours old when one of the new studio nabobs, an ex-junk dealer named Louie Mayer, flashed a contract at Mildred. It was signed. Mildred had a cute face, but was no actress. Mayer, however, saw the salability of billing her as "Mrs. Charlie Chaplin." The contract annoyed Chaplin, who had not been consulted. Mayer announced with great fanfare that the first feature starring Mrs. Charlie Chaplin (Mildred Harris) would be a saga of domestic discord entitled The Inferior Sex.

As a "legit" couple, twenty-nine-year-old Charlie and sixteen-year-old Mildred didn't hit it off too well. Chaplin confided wistfully to Fairbanks that his young with-child bride was "no mental heavyweight." A note

Innocent Mildred Harris ↑   Experienced Peggy Hopkins Joyce ↑   Charlie: A way with women →

of tragedy was injected when Mildred almost died in childbirth; the baby boy was a deformed monster who lived only three days. He was buried in Hollywood Memorial Park Cemetery under a headstone marked "The Little Mouse," with an undertaker's prop smile fixed on his face. He had never smiled.

While Mayer launched a publicity campaign based on "the famous comedian's wife," the Charlie–Mildred marriage went pfft and they began accusing each other (she charged cruelty, he charged infidelity) on the nation's front pages. Chaplin was too discreet to draw attention to the nature of her flights from the conjugal bed — often to spend the night with Metro's "Woman of 1000 Moods," Nazimova. Charlie was also fed up with Mayer's tacky exploitation of his name to promote Mildred's films, the second of which was a "quickie" Mary Pickford imitation titled Polly of the Storm

Country. Given Chaplin's mood, it was evident that sparks would soon fly. A chance encounter occurred April 8, 1920 in the crowded dining room of the fashionable Alexandria Hotel. Seated at opposite tables, Chaplin accused Mayer of encouraging Mildred to up the ante of their divorce settlement. When Mayer stalked out to the hotel's lobby, Chaplin followed. Mayer turned and shouted, "You filthy pervert!"

Chaplin dared him to remove his glasses, upon which Mayer whipped them off with his left and socked Charlie with his right. A solicitous Jack Pickford uprighted Charlie from the potted palm into which he had collapsed and led him away, dripping blood. Mayer, who had learned to scrap during his rough days as a New Brunswick ironmonger, sneered as he watched him go: "I only did what any man would have done."

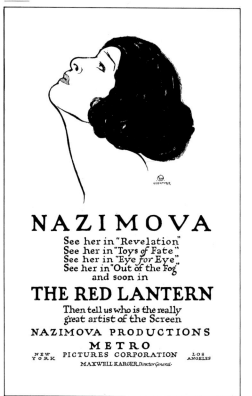

Friend and rival: Pola and Nazimova

Mayer of MGM: Snarls and fisticuffs →

· LO:LITA ·

Then there was the original of that most legendary of nymphets: Lolita.

Who was Lolita? She was born in Hollywood of a Mexican mother and an Irish–American father on April 15, 1908. Her baptismal name was Lillita McMurray. She grew up on the wrong side of Sunset, not far from Chaplin's studio, in a low-rent bungalow. Impudent but not clever, with a broad face and low forehead, she was backward in school.

Chaplin first laid eyes on Lolita when she was seven years old. The year was 1915, the place a popular tearoom frequented by the movie folk, Kitty's Come-On Inn, where Mrs. McMurray (Nana) worked as a waitress. Little Lolita caught Charlie's eye (she knew who he was) and she just simpered and stared. Charlie saw a flimsily-dressed little nuggins with bold eyes. He beckoned her over in an amusing bit of pantomime, asked her name, and soon they were both sharing tea and devil's-food cake served by an observant waitress — Nana.

Before long, Lolita was working as a child extra, and appeared as a flirting angel in the "Heaven" scene in The Kid and as a maid in The Idle Class. Chaplin was helpful, placing Lolita in walk-on parts. With the pay checks coming in for her little girl, Mrs. McMurray could quit her job waiting on tables to devote herself full time to the "education" of her daughter. Nana taught just one course, semester after semester: How To Marry a Millionaire. Dumb Dora finally caught on.

Lolita at twelve, thirteen, fourteen, fifteen — and chicken-hawk Charlie never far away, mistily watching the bud unfold. Lo: Lolita had "filled out" enough to become a leading lady.

Chaplin was launching The Gold Rush, and wouldn't Lolita be fine for the role of the dance-hall girl? Chaplin thought so; Mrs. McMurray exultantly agreed. In March 1924 Lolita signed the contract, jumping up and down and piping "Goody goody!" while pleased Nana looked on. Her daughter was underage, but not too underage, she understood, to spend time off with the boss who was coaching her. (Lolita had been coached at length by Nana on the part she should play with Mr. Chaplin.)

With a militant mother behind her, Lolita at sixteen was suddenly Star of the Chaplin Studios, with her name on Edna Purviance's dressing room door, refurbished to Nana's taste. In honored filmland tradition the

← Chaplin and Lita: Teenage bride

name had been "doctored." Lillita now read LITA and McMurray now read GREY. (Grey was the color and the name of the angora kitten Chaplin had given his young star-mistress — for such she had become — a short time before.) The kitten accompanied Lita to the Chaplin studio, as did her ambitious mother — who never missed a trick.

Press releases praised the new leading lady to the skies for her talent, her beauty, her "aristocratic Spanish forebears," and as The Gold Rush went before the cameras, Chaplin shot miles and miles of film of Lita in the dance-hall scene. It was heavy sledding. In spite of Charlie's infatuation, she didn't photograph well and wouldn't take direction. Whatever Charlie saw in her, a gauche, babyish charm, seemed to evaporate under the hissing kliegs, and all the director's tricks could not restore it. Chaplin began to feel it was the hovering presence of that determined little stage mother, Nana, who kept his bud from blossoming.

Then, one wearying day, on the crowded dance-hall set under the hot kliegs as Lita tried to tango for the umpteenth time, she grabbed her tummy and let out a yell. Thus were the assembled cast and technicians of The Gold Rush company, including the director, informed that Lita was pregnant.

As far as Mrs. McMurray was concerned, watching on the sidelines, the "happy event" had been anticipated. She could now go into her act and scream for the saints in Spanish, and fake a faint. Things were working out according to plan: it was time for uncle Edwin McMurray (conveniently the gentleman was a lawyer) to see Chaplin and point out that premarital sex with an underage female was legally statutory rape.

The subsequent "shotgun marriage" of November 24, 1924 provided the tabloids with their Hollywood Scandal of the Year. It was to be Chaplin's baptism of fire. He sought to avoid scandal, but fifty reporters stampeded after the couple as they fled across the border to Mexico, seeking a quick, anonymous ceremony. Instead they played dusty, heat-wave hide-and-seek with badgering hordes of newsmen.

There was no place to hide in the seedy town of Empalme (state of Sonora) as they entered justice-of-the-peace wedlock with the whole world watching: Charlie Chaplin, thirty-five, and his pregnant bride, sixteen. Lita's mother and uncle were there . . . to make sure the groom did not take a powder. Quite a story.

The tabloids recorded that as the newlyweds fought their way through the posse of reporters, Chaplin looked "grey." Parrying impertinent questions with his "prop" smile, he reached his limousine with Lita and made a getaway, scattering newshounds in the dust. While groom and nymph were border-bound, a Hearst feature writer was phoning in his "exclusive" on the wedding chase across the badlands.

Joining a group of friends for the wedding-night train trip back to L.A., Chaplin was heard to remark, "Well, boys, this is better than the penitentiary but it won't last."

When the headlines of CHARLIE AND HIS CHILD BRIDE hit the nation, Lita Grey, who wore wings for a "bit" in The Kid and had shot miles of unusable scenes for The Gold Rush, was as well known as any Hollywood star. With her pregnant marriage, however, she "retired from the screen."

Retirement was to offer Lita

Lita and sons →

88

and the rest of the McMurray clan "compensations." Nana was at work behind the scenes to assure that the screen career her little girl was giving up would be replaced by something more solid. She and uncle Ed estimated that Chaplin had assets worth $16,000,000.

On their return to Chaplin's forty-room Beverly Hills mansion the newlyweds were accompanied across the threshold by Nana. Like a nightmare mother-in-law joke Mrs. McMurray invited herself in and made herself at home . . . for two harrowing years. (Ma-in-law used the pretext that Lita was still a "child" and could not manage the household.)

The papers noted the birth of a son, Charles Spencer Chaplin, Jr., on June 28, 1925, seven months

after the marriage. A second son, Sydney Earle Chaplin, was born March 30, 1926, just nine months and two days later. By this time Chaplin's home was no longer his own. The McMurray Clan of Beverly Hills hillbillies had taken over, and large, rowdy drinking parties were the rule. On the night of December 1, 1926, Chaplin returned home after a difficult day's work on The Circus, to find a drunken circus had taken over his house. The inevitable explosion occurred, and after an exchange of wrathful words, Lita packed up the two babies and exited with her entourage of drunken guests and the McMurray Clan.

By the time Lita filed for divorce on January 10, 1927, the diabolic mother–daughter "money plot" had long since dawned on Chaplin. By then it was too late. The dynamic duo relinquished their grip for a price: a cool million. During those two years of married hell, little Lolita metamorphosed into ferocious Xanthippe, stage managed by Nana. Chaplin's every move in the house, every exit and entrance that smacked of peccadillo, every free-thinking remark or intimate suggestion shared with his wife in bed were reported by daughter and noted down by mother in a big business ledger. Nana then turned over the evidence to uncle Ed, the lawyer in the family.

When Chaplin fled, breaking off work on The Circus and fleeing to the home of Nathan Burkan, his New York attorney, all of his property was seized by the legal team headed by uncle Ed. Chaplin suffered a nervous breakdown in New York and was treated in the Burkan home by Dr. Gustav Tiek, an eminent nerve specialist. When restored to sanity, Chaplin was dismayed to learn that the entire country had

← Chaplin in The Idle Class: Expensive extras, Mrs. McMurray and Lita as maids been inundated by salacious reading matter distilled from his two years of married hell.

Printed in pamphlet form, forty-two pages long, titled Complaint by Lita Grey, the spicy little item that had all the Sheiks and Shebas buzzing was nothing other than a transcription of "Lita Grey Chaplin's BILL OF DIVORCEMENT from Charles Spencer Chaplin." This had been leaked to a clandestine scandal press by Lita's lawyers at the moment the petition was filed. This smear job sold tens of thousands of copies at a quarter each in a few weeks.

Sprinkled through the legalese was a Latin term, fellatio, that had quite a few flappers heading for a dictionary. It seems Mrs. Chaplin did not want to perform this "abnormal, against nature, perverted, degenerate and indecent act" (as described by Lita's lawyers) while Chaplin encouraged her, "Relax, dear — all married people do it."

According to the Complaint, from the time she became intimate with him, "the Respondent never had marital relations with the Plaintiff in the manner that is usual between husband and wife." (This rather begs the question of how she managed to conceive.)

During the divorce proceedings, the two baby boys were brandished before judge and photographers in a

great display of motherly love.

The grievances against Chaplin enumerated in the Complaint came under five principal headings:

1. The Plaintiff was seduced by the Respondent.
2. The Respondent requested the Plaintiff to submit to an abortion when the condition of conception was confirmed.
3. The Respondent did not consent to marry the Plaintiff except after being constrained and forced to do so, and then with the reservation of the intention of divorce.
4. To precipitate the divorce the Respondent subjected the

The McMurray Clan: Calculating ↑

Plaintiff to a calculated plan of cruel and inhuman treatment.

5. The merits of these claims is proven by the immorality of everyday conversation of Charles Chaplin, by his theories concerning the most sacred subjects, which he holds in contempt.

In illustration of the fifth charge, Lita cited several conversations in which Chaplin made light of the institution of marriage and the sex laws of the state of California. In his persistent effort to "undermine and corrupt her moral impulses, to demoralize her rules of decency," Chaplin even read Lita passages from "immoral" literature such as Lady Chatterley's Lover.

Another effort at enlightenment proved equally unacceptable: "Whereas, four months before the separation of the Plaintiff and the Respondent, the Respondent suggested that a young girl who had the reputation of performing acts of sexual perversity spend the evening at their home, and the Respondent told the Plaintiff that they could 'have some fun together.'"

When she nixed this proposal, she testified that Chaplin, exasperated, shouted at her, "Just you wait. I'll blow my top one of these days, and I'll kill you!"

For his part, Chaplin issued the following statement to the press: "I married Lita Grey because I loved her and, like many other foolish men, I loved her more when she wronged me and I am afraid I still love her. I was stunned and ready for suicide that day when she told me that she didn't love me but that we must marry. Lita's mother often suggested to me that I marry Lita, and I said I would love to if only we could have children. I thought I was incapable of fatherhood. Her mother deliberately and continuously put Lita in my path. She encouraged our relations."

Not all press reaction was against Chaplin. H. L. Mencken commented in the Baltimore Sun: "The very morons who worshipped Charlie Chaplin six weeks ago now prepare to dance around the stake while he is burned; he is learning something of the psychology of the mob . . . A public trial involving sexual accusations is made a carnival everywhere in the United States . . ."

Lita's clique sensed a turn of the tide in favor of Chaplin, so decided to play their trump. They threatened to name, in court, "five prominent motion-picture actresses" with whom Chaplin had been intimate during his marriage.

That did it. To prevent the names of these actresses being dragged into the case (particularly that of Marion Davies, who had offered Chaplin refuge at Ocean House on numerous nights when things got too rough at home) Chaplin capitulated. A cash settlement was agreed upon, and Lita changed her sensational complaint to a single charge of cruelty.

On August 22, 1927, after "acting" on the stand for twenty minutes, Lita was awarded a $625,000 settlement. A shaken Chaplin returned to Hollywood to resume work on The Circus, interrupted for a year by the litigation. He was a bachelor once more, but an embittered clown. He confided to his cameraman, Rollie Totheroh: "What I've been through has aged me ten years." To resume his role it was necessary for Chaplin to dye his hair black; like the survivor of the Maelstrom, his encounter with Lilith-Lita had turned his hair white.

It was only natural that Lita should split her bounty with the "manager" of the show: Nana.

Chaplin: Morose witness →

·WILLIAM RANDOLPH'S·
·HEARSE·

The very month of Chaplin's disastrous marriage to Lita Grey, Hollywood was treated to another scorcher. This one also intimately involved good old Charlie — with an all-star supporting cast. It would have sold lots of papers. Just one headline appeared: MOVIE PRODUCER SHOT ON HEARST YACHT. This story in the Los Angeles Times was yanked in later editions. Something was going on — a gigantic cover-up.

William Randolph Hearst, lugubrious lord of the press, was the reason. He was so feared that not even rival tabloids would risk an open affront to the redoutable "W.R." Although his association with Marion Davies was notorious, at no time were their names linked publicly in the papers. Hearst's $400,000,000 silver-mine fortune made money talk on a colossal scale. The fourth estate had heard tales of certain newsmen being barred from further employment after displeasing him. Even though word of the liaison had reached some of the country's most ruthless yellow sheets, for once the tabs decided to let a "natural" pass.

Hearst set up Cosmopolitan Productions for the greater glory of Marion Davies — a vanity operation if ever there was one. His papers and magazines incessantly proclaimed her the greatest miracle the movies had ever seen; a huge Georgian barn on the beach at Santa Monica was erected by Willie's wand to house his winsome mistress. Marion's "Beach House" parties were the most extravagant the movie colony had ever seen; the Golden People grabbed at the chance of an invitation to the Hearst affairs, and gave Marion good marks as a hostess even if privately they made fun of her attempts at histrionics on the screen.

To vary the entertainment, Hearst brought his 280-foot yacht Oneida (formerly a floating palace for the Kaiser) through the Panama Canal and kept it anchored at San Pedro. Invitations to the intimate festivities on board the barge were even more sought after than those for the spectacular "Beach House" parties.

The cream of Hollywood's charmed circle received Hearst's invitation to a cruise of the Oneida scheduled to depart November 15, 1924 for a jaunt to San Diego. The occasion was celebrating the forty-third birthday of Thomas H. Ince, a pioneer producer–director, "Father of the Western." Hearst was in the midst of negotiations with Ince to use his Culver City studio as a base for

---

Cosmopolitan. Among the fifteen guests were several friends of Ince, including his business manager, George H. Thomas, and his mistress, actress Margaret Livingston. (Wife Nell would not be there.) Other guests included British authoress Elinor Glyn; actresses Aileen Pringle, Seena Owen, and Julanna Johnston; Dr. Daniel Carson Goodman, production head of Cosmopolitan; Joseph Willicombe, Hearst's chief secretary; Frank Barham, the publisher, and wife; Marion's sisters Ethel and Reine and Marion's niece, Pepi.

Marion Davies was collected on the set of Zander the Great at United Artists by two other guests, Charlie Chaplin and a Hearst movie columnist from New York, Louella O. Parsons, on her first visit to Hollywood. They all drove down together to San Pedro.

The Oneida took to sea with a cargo of celebrities, a jazz band, a stock of vintage champagne and twenty-seven-year-old Marion and sixty-two-year-old Big Daddy as hostess and host. Skipper Hearst set a southern route, passing Catalina and swinging down toward San Diego and Baja.

Tom Ince, the guest of honor, missed the boat. He had to attend the première of his latest production, The Mirage, and agreed to take the last train down to San Diego, where he would board the Oneida when it docked.

The birthday party on board is said to have been great fun — up to a point. Beyond that point, the Oneida sailed straight into a fog bank of conflicting stories.

The "official" version as released by Hearst House couldn't be

---

Marion Davies in a Hearst production, The Red Mill ↑

more simple: poor Tom Ince glutted himself with rich Hearstian hospitality at his Scorpio Birthday Party and died of acute indigestion.

The first story to appear in the Hearst papers was a preposterous fake:

SPECIAL CAR RUSHES STRICKEN MAN HOME FROM RANCH.

"Ince, with his wife, Nell, and his two young sons, had been visiting William Randolph Hearst at his upstate ranch for several days previous to the attack. When the illness came upon him suddenly the film magnate, stricken unconscious, was removed to a special car attended by two specialists and three nurses, and hurried back to his canyon home. His wife and sons, and his brothers, Ralph and John, were at his bedside when the end came."

Unfortunately for Hearst, witnesses had seen Ince board the yacht at San Diego. Even more regrettable, Kono, Chaplin's secretary, saw a bullet hole in Ince's head as he was carried off the Oneida. Acute indigestion?

Hearst kept a diamond-studded revolver aboard the yacht for the purposes of a singular entertainment, considering that he was publicly known as an anti-vivisectionist. As John Tebbel relates, Hearst was an expert shot: "It amused him to surprise guests on the Oneida by knocking down a seagull with a quick hip shot."

Hearst was also uncommonly jealous of other men's attentions to Marion; detectives had kept him informed of her dalliance with Chaplin during his absence. Chaplin had been invited so that Hearst could observe his comportment with Marion.

Chaplin may have had some qualms about going, but decided to put up a good show. He left his pregnant fiancée, Lita, behind.

It is believed that during the birthday party Hearst noticed that Marion and Charlie had slipped off together and were later discovered by Hearst in flagrante on the lower deck. In her famous stutter, Marion let out a prophetic scream — "M-m-m-murder!" — which brought the other guests running as Hearst ran for his revolver. In the ensuing confusion, Ince, not Chaplin, dropped, a bullet in his brain.

Ince's funeral was held in Hollywood on November 21, attended by his family, Marion Davies, Charlie Chaplin, Mary Pickford, Douglas Fairbanks and Harold Lloyd. Hearst was conspicuously absent. The body was immediately cremated.

It is notable that no official inquest into the death of Tom Ince had been held. With the "evidence" in ashes, Hearst thought he had the grisly

Aileen Pringle: Mute witness ↑

situation well in hand.

He hadn't counted on the Hollywood rumor mill. In spite of the fact that everyone on board the Oneida, guests and crew alike, had been sworn to secrecy, persistent rumors linked Ince's death with Hearst. Was this another case of a rich man getting away with murder?

The rumors finally prompted San Diego's District Attorney, Chester Kemply, to call for an investigation. Strangely, of all the guests and crew on board the Oneida, only Dr. Daniel Carson Goodman, who was Hearst's employee, was called to testify. This is his story:

On Saturday November 15th I took the Oneida, which belongs to International Film Corporation, with a party on board, to San Diego. Mr. Ince was to have been one of the party. He was unable to leave Saturday, stating that he had to work, but would join us Sunday morning.

When he arrived on board he complained of nothing but being tired. Ince discussed during the day details of his agreement just made with International Film Corporation to produce pictures in combination. Ince seemed well. He ate a hearty dinner, retired early. Next morning he and I arose early before any of the other guests to return to Los Angeles. Ince complained that during the night he had had an attack of indigestion, and still felt bad. On the way to the station he complained of a pain in the heart. We boarded the train, but at Del Mar a heart attack came upon him. I thought it best to take him off the train, insist upon his resting in a hotel. I telephoned Mrs. Ince that her husband was not feeling well. I called in a physician and remained myself until the afternoon, when I continued on to Los Angeles.

Mr. Ince told me that he had had similar attacks before, but that they had not amounted to anything. Mr. Ince gave no evidence of having had any liquor of any kind. My knowledge as a physician enabled me to diagnose the case as one of acute indigestion.

The San Diego D.A. then dismissed the case with these words:

I began this investigation because of many rumors brought to my office regarding the case, and have considered them until today in order to definitely dispose of them. There will be no further investigation of stories of drinking on board the yacht. If there are to be, then they will have to be in Los Angeles County where presumably the liquor was secured. People interested in Ince's sudden death have continued to come to me with persistent reports and in order to satisfy them I did conduct an investigation. But after questioning the doctor and nurse

who attended Mr. Ince at Del Mar I am satisfied his death was from ordinary causes.

This dismissal left an editorialist of the Long Beach News dissatisfied:

At the risk of losing something of a reputation as a prophet, the writer will predict that some day one of the scandal-scented mysteries in filmdom will be cleared up. Motion picture circles have suffered alike from scandal and rumors of scandal. Deaths from violence or mysterious sources have been hinted at but never proved. If there is any foundation for suspicioning that Thomas Ince's death was from other than natural causes an investigation should be made in justice to the public as well as to those concerned.

If there was liquor aboard a millionaire's yacht in San Diego Harbor, where Ince was taken ill, it should be investigated. A District Attorney who passes up the matter because he sees "no reason" to investigate is the best agent Bolshevists could employ in this country.

It was understood that District Attorney Kemply's investigation was to establish what had actually occurred at the party directly preceding the director's death. The probe halted before any members of the party had even been questioned.

Some thought it no coincidence that Louella Parsons was awarded a lifetime contract with Hearst soon after this incident, with her syndication expanded. It was rumored she had seen it all. Louella soon felt obliged to do a little covering up of her own, and claimed she had been in New York at the time. The only inconvenience was that Marion's stand-in, Vera Burnett, clearly recalled seeing Louella with Davies and Chaplin at the studio, ready for departure. (Vera valued her job and decided not to insist upon it.)

The Hearst–Davies diarchy rode out the scandal unscathed, but as D.W. Griffith remarked in later years, "All you have to do to make Hearst turn white as a ghost is mention Ince's name. There's plenty wrong there, but Hearst is too big to touch."

It was known throughout the film colony that the mention of Ince's name within Hearst's hearing would nix future invitations to the Santa Monica beach house or the San Simeon castle.

And there l'affaire Ince remains today, still shrouded in mystery, still subject to speculation.

A perverse footnote concerning Ince became known to the film colony when his widow put his home up for sale after her husband's death. This was the enormous Spanish-style mansion, Días Doradas, in Benedict Canyon, which Ince had designed himself — a showplace where the Golden People delighted to spend frolicsome weekends. The charmed circle ignored one naughty feature: a secret gallery above the guest rooms provided with concealed peepholes, revealing a fine view of each bed. Some of Hollywood's most celebrated couples had thus repaid their host's bounty by a gracious demonstration of their boudoir techniques. Only Peeping Tom Ince had the key to the concealed passageway.

Hearst discreetly provided Ince's widow, Nell, with a trust fund. The Depression wiped out the fund, and Nell finished her days as a taxi driver.

And Hearst? The entire affair was reduced to a sardonic joke in the film colony — the Oneida became known as "William Randolph's Hearse."

Marion and Willie →

·RUDY'S REP·

The next flood of scandalous rumors to hit Hollywood had a similar mortuary overtone. The occasion was the death of the screen's "Great Lover," Rudolph Valentino, on August 23, 1926, at ten minutes after noon, in New York's Polyclinic Hospital.

The official cause of death was stated to be peritonitis, following an operation for an inflamed appendix. But rumor attributed his death to an "arsenic revenge" by a well-known New York society woman, whom he dropped after a brief affair, while in the city on a personal appearance tour to promote his last film, The Son of the Sheik. Other rumors affirmed Rudy had been shot by an irate husband, or that the star was syphilitic and died when the disease struck the brain.

During the last years of his life, the dream lover of millions of women had been the butt of a number of unkind attacks in the nation's newspapers, ranging from sneers at his testimonials for Valvoline Face Cream, to remarks that cast a doubt on his virility.

The unkindest cut of all came from an editorial writer for the Chicago Tribune, who chose the moment of Rudy's personal appearance in that city to issue a broadside. The July 18, 1926 editorial of "The World's Greatest Newspaper" gouged

Valentino in no uncertain terms:

PINK POWDER PUFFS
A new public ballroom was opened on the north side a few days ago, a truly handsome place and apparently well run. The pleasant impression lasts until one steps into the men's washroom and finds there on the wall a contraption of glass tubes and levers and a slot for the insertion of a coin. The glass tubes contain a fluffy pink solid, and beneath them one reads an amazing legend which runs something like this: "Insert coin. Hold personal puff beneath the tube. Then pull the lever."

A powder vending machine! In a men's washroom! Homo Americanus! Why didn't someone quietly drown Rudolph Gugliemo, alias Valentino, years ago?

And was the pink powder machine pulled from the wall and ignored? It was not. It was used. We personally saw two "men" — as young lady contributors to the Voice of the People are wont to describe the breed — step up, insert coin, hold kerchief beneath the spout, pull the lever, then take the pretty pink stuff and pat it on their cheeks in front of the mirror.

Another member of this department, one of the most benevolent men

---

← Valentino on the set of Blood and Sand: Evident virility

on earth, burst raging into the office
the other day because he had
seen a young "man" combing his
pomaded hair in the elevator.
But we claim our pink powder story
beats his all hollow.

It is time for a matriarchy if the male
of the species allows such things
to persist. Better a rule by masculine
women than by effeminate men.
Man began to slip, we are beginning to
believe, when he discarded the
straight razor for the safety pattern.
We shall not be surprised when
we hear that the safety razor has given
way to the depilatory.

Who or what is to blame is what
puzzles me. Is this degeneration into
effeminacy a cognate reaction
with pacifism to the virilities and realities
of the war? Are pink powder and
parlor pinks in any way related? How
does one reconcile masculine
cosmetics, sheiks, floppy pants, and
slave bracelets with a disregard
for law and an aptitude for crime more
in keeping with the frontier of half
a century ago than a twentieth-century
metropolis?

Do women like the type of "man"

who pats pink powder on his face in a
public washroom and arranges
his coiffure in a public elevator? Do
women at heart belong to the
Wilsonian era of "I Didn't Raise My
Boy to Be a Soldier"? What has
become of the old "caveman" line?

It is a strange social phenomenon
and one that is running its course
not only here in America but in Europe
as well. Chicago may have its
powder puffs; London has its dancing
men and Paris its gigolos. Down
with Decatur; up with Elinor Glyn.
Hollywood is the national school of
masculinity. Rudy, the beautiful
gardener's boy, is the prototype of the
American male.

Hell's bells. Oh, sugar.

Rudy hardly thought it sporting
he should be blamed for the
mannerisms of a bunch of young
Clark Street faggots, and furiously
challenged the Tribune hatchet
man to a duel or even a fist fight. This
and similar attacks found their
origin in Valentino's well-known taste
for sartorial extravagance, his
famous slave bracelet without which
he was never seen in public, his
gold jewelry and preference for heavy
perfumes, chinchilla-lined coats
and pronounced Italianate coquetry.

His virility was further impugned
when it became known that the
women he married were both lesbians.

When Natacha Rambova,
Valentino's second wife (whose slave
bracelet he wore at all times),
divorced him in 1926, it was revealed
that the marriage had not been
consummated.

A similar charge had been advanced
during divorce proceedings with
his first wife, Jean Acker, in 1922. She
accused him of slighting her in
the sexual department and of slugging
her as well.

Rudy married his second lesbian

Rudy with Nazimova in Camille: Lesbian marriage-broker →

108

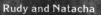
Rudy and Natacha

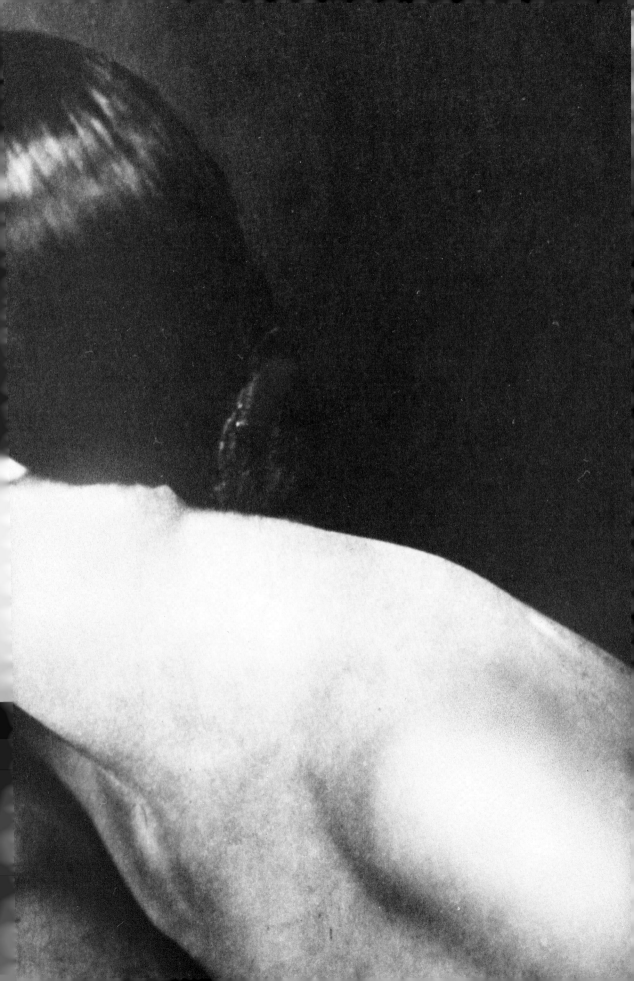

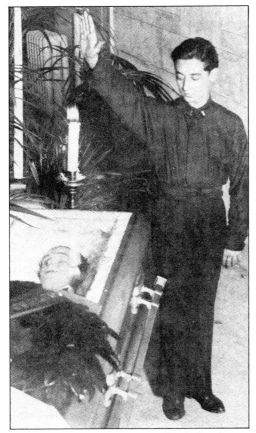

While Rudy may have been maneuvered into matrimony with an assist from Alla, there is no doubt he sought women stronger than himself and was attracted to "butch" ladies. Valentino called Natacha "The Boss" and she lived up to the name so well—constantly high-handing her husband's career at Paramount — that Zukor resorted to a contract with a clause barring her from the set. She retaliated by ordering Rudy to leave Paramount. She then wrote a screenplay for Valentino, The Hooded Falcon, which proved "unproducible" after a considerable investment in time and money. One collaboration of Natacha and Rudy saw the light of day; a slim volume of verse entitled Daydreams, whose closing lines are:

Alas
  At times
  I find
Exquisite bitterness
In
  Your kiss.

Whatever his private accommodations with his virile wives may have been, the public slurs on his manhood caused him such bitterness that even as he lay dying, fighting stoically against terrible pain, he asked the physicians at his bedside: "And now, do I act like a pink powder puff?"

At the news of Valentino's death, two women attempted suicide in front of Polyclinic Hospital; in London a girl took poison before Rudy's inscribed photograph; an elevator boy of the Ritz in Paris was found dead on a bed covered with Valentino's photos.

While Valentino was lying in state at Campbell's Funeral Home, New York streets became the scene of a ghoulish carnival as a mob

before his divorce decree from his first was final. This oversight led to his arrest for bigamy.

Both Jean Acker and Natacha Rambova were "protégées" of the exotic and equally lesbian actress Alla Nazimova — Hollywood's most distinguished feminine import at that time — whose Bohemian gatherings at her famous Sunset Boulevard estate, The Garden of Allah, caused considerable comment. It was Natacha who designed the Beardsleyesque costumes for Alla's own production of Salome, in which Nazimova starred herself, employed only homosexual actors as "homage" to Wilde, and lost her shirt. Matchmaker Alla introduced Rudy to both his wives, and was believed in Hollywood to have stage managed both marriages — erratically, to judge by the results.

THERE'S A NEW STAR
IN HEAVEN TO-NIGHT

RUDOLPH VALENTINO

by
J. Keirn Brennan
writer of "A Little Bit Of Heaven" etc.
Irving Mills
and
Jimmy McHugh

of over 100,000 fought for a last glimpse of the Great Lover. The body was flanked by phony Fascist Black Shirt guards at attention, with an equally phony wreath labeled "From Benito" nearby — a press-agent stunt by Campbell's whose cosmeticians really made Rudy's corpse resemble a "pink powder puff."

Among those who won admittance to the candle-lit bier were his ex-wife Jean Acker, whose display of grief at the coffin's edge might have been tempered had she known Rudy left her a solitary dollar in his will, and Pola Negri, who upstaged everybody by rushing in from Hollywood decked out in chic-est mourning weeds. She sobbed and fainted before the coffin . . . and the photographers. Between sobs, Pola claimed she had promised her hand to Rudy. Another claim was immediately filed in the papers by Ziegfeld Girl Marion Kay Brenda, who stated Valentino had proposed to her in Texas Guinan's night club the evening before he was stricken.

As Rudy's body was shipped West for entombment in the Court of the Apostles of Hollywood Memorial Park Cemetery, a commemorative song was crooned by Rudy Vallee over the nation's radios: "There's a New Star in Heaven Tonight — R-u-d-y V-a-l-e-n-t-i-n-o."

Valentino's demise at thirty-one left inconsolable paramours of both sexes, to judge by the tear-streaked testimonials. Aside from the "Lady in Black" bearing flowers annually to the mausoleum on the anniversary of his death, the memory of Rudy was cherished by Ramon Novarro, who kept a black lead Art Deco dildo embellished with Valentino's silver signature in a bedroom shrine. A present from Rudy.

Valentino memorial in DeLongpre Park, Hollywood ↑   The "Lady in Black" →

· THE DIRTY HUN ·

Another perennial source of scandalous rumor in Hollywood during the Twenties revolved on the question of what really went on during the shooting of the notorious "orgy scenes" in the films of that stormy individualist, Erich von Stroheim.

There was ample room for speculation as the deluxe bordello sequences directed by Stroheim for Merry-Go-Round, The Merry Widow, The Wedding March and the unfinished Queen Kelly were all closely guarded conclaves, on stages where even the studio chiefs were "off limits."

It is no wonder these sessions under the hot kliegs were considered to be not just make-believe but veritable Lupercalia.

Shooting sometimes continued for twenty hours without pause on the locked stages. Stroheim "treated" the participants to squab and caviar and served real champagne in spite of Prohibition. The hand-picked extras — exotic women and aristocratic types, many of whom were genuine émigrés — often emerged with the look of having spent a weekend in Sodom, bleary-eyed and staggering. Some girls, teetering on the edge of hysterics, bore evidence of whip marks or bites.

Stroheim saw to it these extras were handsomely rewarded for the hours of overtime; they respected their director's law of silence once off the closed set.

Stroheim often devoted weeks of work and considerable chunks of Universal, Paramount and Metro-Goldwyn-Mayer money, as well as the personal fortunes of Gloria Swanson and Joseph Kennedy, filming wild scenes of Alt Wien decadence that no censor in the world at that time would have passed — certainly not Will Hays with his prim Purity Code of "Don'ts" and "Be Carefuls."

Since the complete rushes of this orgy footage were only seen by a few of Von's cronies and the horrified studio bosses hacked the scenes to shreds to comply with Hays' strictures (the censors would then make their additional cuts so that only a few teasing flashes from the orgies remained in the release prints), imagination ran riot as to what actually had gone on.

It was believed that the "show" being watched with such avidity through a row of peepholes in The Wedding March really was worth peeping for.

It was known that for just one scene in this same film Stroheim imported a professional lady sadist from Vienna, skilled in the

application of the "spider."

The fancy brothel of <u>The Wedding March</u> had featured whores of all races, each with her erotic specialty; the fairies in white wigs and white body make-up who played stringed instruments had been blindfolded to prevent recognition of the "nobs" present. The chastity belts of the Negro "slaves" were sealed with heart-shaped padlocks; one refinement due more to Stroheim's imagination than Austria-Hungary's depravity was a pretty pair of accommodating Siamese twins!

It is suspected Stroheim was burning

<u>The Merry Widow</u>: Fatal shoe fetish

Director and Leading Lady Mae did not get along →

up MGM money with malice aforethought on such unshowable scenes in revenge for the destruction of the miles of negative of his epic study in avarice, Greed, by his mortal enemies, Irving Thalberg, production chief of MGM, and its new boss, Louie Mayer.

Thalberg earned Stroheim's enmity in 1923, when the former was production manager at Universal, and took the direction of Merry-Go-Round away from Von after he had indulged in a series of wild extravagances such as ordering silk underdrawers with the monogram of the Imperial Guard for the Guardsmen in the film.

In spite of the fact that his MGM film, The Merry Widow, was a subsequent box-office smash, the fanatic scruples of Stroheim were not made to please the likes of Mayer and Thalberg. They set out to "get" him and spread the word around town that Von was an untrustworthy wastrel, "uncommercial" and a sex maniac. The legend of his extravagance, which began as a publicity stunt at Universal when his name had been written "$troheim" during the shooting of Foolish Wives, eventually boomeranged; Von now had difficulty finding backers. The front-office men echoed from studio to studio that "working with Stroheim was like shoveling dollars down a well."

The saga of Stroheim in Hollywood — the battle of a giant against pygmies — was doomed to end badly. The little minds of the front-office men got the better of this ferocious visionary.

After his disenchanted return to Europe, Erich von Stroheim declared: "Hollywood killed me." That was the least Hollywood could do to the most disconcerting genius who ever challenged its cardboard dogmas.

Queen Kelly: Unfinished masterpiece ↑   **Stroheim and his beloved celluloid →**

· HOLLYWOOD HEADLINES ·

Whether the power behind the press happened to be Big Daddy Hearst, with his redolent rotten-apple yellow sheet, the Mirror; his gutter competitor Bernard Macfadden and his wildly fibbing GraphiC or just some fever-brained, small-town editor trying to make a go of it, the pulp-and-ink wiseacres all knew HOLLYWOOD HEADLINES SOLD NEWSPAPERS — if they were Spicy! Shocking!! or Downright Scandalous!!!

For all Hays might whine on in his Hoosier twang, in appeals for the papers to report film colony news "fairly," the press devoted much more space to Hollywood's fourteen top-name divorces and three separations for the year 1926, for instance, than it did to the twenty-three stellar marriages of that same year.

Canon Chase, one of the Twenties' more pushy professional prudes, was overjoyed when word leaked out in 1926 that Will Hays had taken payola from Harry "Teapot Dome" Sinclair while a member of Harding's Cabinet. Chase lashed out in the press at Hollywood and Hays, claiming Celluloid City was just as indecent as ever and implying that he could do a nippier job in the clean-up department.

Hays maintained a prim silence under this competitor of the cloth's frontal assault. He was busy seeing to it that the nation's churches received notice of Hollywood's holier-than-thou intentions in Cecil B. DeMille's superpious King of Kings, a forthcoming screen sermon, and that H.B. Warner, the queen who played the Christus, drank not, neither would he smoke or swear. Moreover, the Virgin Mary would have to forget about her plans for divorce.

In spite of these unctuous handouts the press continued its wicked anti-Hollywood bias as the Twenties played itself out. The groundwork had been laid with the Arbuckle–Taylor–Reid scandals, topped by the salacious tales leaked out to the nation during Chaplin's sticky split from Lita Grey.

If the tabs needed something "grabbing" for a weekend edition — if the Hall-Mills or Snyder-Gray mayhem was running thin, or if Daddy Browning & Peaches were beginning to pall — there was always an "exposé" of some new vice or peril to America's girlhood in Hollywood, City of Sin. There was always some disillusioned "Beauty Queen" around who hadn't made it, willing to tell the world that she had been "ruined" by the movie minions — for her picture on page one and a price.

The image was also helped along by

← Louella and Hedda: A Witches' Brew

Mae Murray, who sold her sensational "memoirs" to be serialized in Hearst's folk-surrealist Sunday supplement, The American Weekly. One juicy installment entitled "The Dirtiest Hun in Hollywood" embroidered on her on-set row with Stroheim during the MGM lensing of The Merry Widow.

Middle America of a Sunday morning was titillated to learn that "The Man You Love To Hate" was indeed a reel-life monster. So sadistic was he that Princess Mae (She of the Bee-Stung Lips) was driven to shout in front of 1000 fancy-dress extras, "You dirty hun!" and stalk off the Chez Maxim's set. When star-reporter Murray tattled that the studio boss, Louis Bollocks Mayer, chopped Stroheim on the kisser while Boy Genius Iggy Thalberg counted Vile Von out to the stroke of ten on Louie's Culver City carpet, the nuclear family readers were led to assume it all had something to do with L.B.M.'s gallantry. The fact was that Stroheim had let drop within Yiddisher Momist Mayer's hearing that in Kaiser Von's opinion, "All vimmen are whores!" (Beet-faced Louie did indeed unleash his terrible swift haymaker upon Bullet Head, screaming to his phalanx of yesperson private secretaries, "No vun kin talk about vimmen like dat in my presence und git away vit it!")

All through the twittish Twenties the tabs trotted out the oldie but goodie Hollywood Filth Parade, drooling oceans of ink over WILD PARTIES IN PICTURELAND,

Visiting Gossipist Elsa Maxwell: Hollywood genuflects ↑   Clara Bow →

TRYING "TO

GET THERE"

WEEKEND ORGIES OF THE STARS OF THE SILVER SHEET, SINGED STARLET WARNS OF WINDING CELLULOID ROAD TO RUIN, or MOVIELAND MASHERS SET THEIR SNARES. The sex-teased, sensation-thirsty, straphanger-shopgirl public lapped it up and dished out its pennies for more.

That public's craving for a nonstop movie-star titillation fix was mainlined and bylined day by day by that syndicated, sob-sister, mutant, deadlining hunt-and-pecker: the Hollywood Gossip Columnist. The dwarf ancestor of all Ronas was of course the original, panting, go-getting Paganini of Piffle, Louella "Oneida" (I-Saw-What-You-Did!) Parsons, set up by W.R. as Chief Hearst Hollywood Correspondent.

Lumpen-Pate Louella! Lollipop's daily morning prattle column told the breakfasting nation the scoop-by-scoop Hollywood Score, the Who's-Fucking-Who-Stakes Out West Where Fortunes Grow. Lolly called it "going out" together, but

the flappers knew what that naughty-naughty meant. The great gee-whiz public out there could also thank Lolly for spilling the steaming beans on who was Hollywood-IN and who was Hollywood-OUT — the Dread Exiled State indicated by pointed column exclusion or a Lollypudlian avalanche of abuse — if Pitiless Parsons of Parvenu Parish, on her own twit, or prompted by Pope William's iron whim, felt stung to vengeance.

While pushy L.O.P. and her legion of copycat peddlers teased the newsprint nationwide, the smart-ass big-city tabs offered ranker meat: for the GraphiC & Co there was No Badder Place than Hollywood — Reborn BABYLON, with Santa Monica–Sodom and Glendale–Gomorrah for suburbs. The tattlemen luridly depicted the Stars as glittering soulless women wandering from wicked to wanton orgy on the tuxed arms of vainglorious males of malevolent beauty, in a moneyed, perfumed world haunted by the specters of Drink, Dope

← Lolly Parsons: Paganini of Piffle

and Debauchery, Insanity, Suicide, and Murder. While in the Sodom-Gomorrah suburbs, the Lavender Swamp, ways of sinning took place that were certainly weirder, it was hinted, than fornication and adultery. The straphangers got their three-cents-worth.

It is true that from the time it became the Motion Picture Capital of the World, shady characters descended on boom-town Hollywood like swarms of moths drawn to a searchlight. Two-bit gangsters, 'leggers, pushers, hard-sell swindlers, blackmailers, burglars, gross and petty extortionists, all manner of ultrakinky sex freaks, dummy-stock speculators, crank cultists, dollar astrologists, fake mediums and epicene evangelists, phony healers, crooked fortunetellers and parasitic "psychoanalysts." All of them fluttered graspingly about the edges of the charmed circle.

Thousands of green, dumb young screen-struck kids were lured by the hollow promises of phony talent schools — a Hollywood Fool's Gold Rush that panned out nothing but bitter dross. Many pretty-faced patsies, deluded of dreams and empty of pocket, drifted into prostitution.

These newly-recruited L.A. streetwalkers called themselves "movie extras" to avoid the California vagrancy laws. If they were raked in by the Vice Squad or raided in cheap hotels, the nation's papers escalated the incident: BEAUTIFUL FILM STARS NABBED IN HOUSE OF ILL FAME. Hot-eyed reporters would then describe a Luscious Brunette, Stunning Blonde or Knockout Redhead. Their names were "withheld" in order to allow the reader to flesh out in his imagination dusky Dolores Del Rio, blonde Alice White or Hollywood's hottest redhead, Clara Bow.

Hollywood Harem: "Movie extras" ↑   "Film Star Nabbed" →

· CLARA'S BEAUX ·

It must be added that Clara — known since 1926 as the "Hottest Jazz Baby in Films" — soon had her own headlines across the country's front pages.

The tabloids screamed:

CLARA'S "LOVE BALM" ROMANCE,

and the avid readers learned that the prolonged "therapy" she had been receiving for "nerves" and "insomnia" from Hollywood's most expensive and dashing society physician, bedside-mannered Dr. William Earl Pearson, consisted in the repeated application of Dr. Pearson's arrow on the naked prostrate Bow. The "love balm" was rubbed in on a nightly basis until Pearson's wife put a private eye on her medic husband's tail. The trail ended in the Chinese Den of Clara's Beverly Hills hacienda.

Clara lost some sleep when Mrs. Pearson named her corespondent in a divorce petition, suing La Bow for "alienation of affections." The tabs squeezed every drop of juice out of the "love balm" scandal featuring Hollywood's hottest jazz baby, and Clara was soaked for $30,000 by the Good Doc's neglected spouse.

Clara moved on to run up spectacular front-page Reno gambling debts. But her hottest scandal did not erupt until 1930.

In 1930 Clara's trusted private secretary, Daisy DeVoe, an Eve Harringtonish bright-faced blonde, sold all the ins and outs of the "It" Girl's nonstop love life during four frenzied years to the highest paying tabloid, New York's quasi-porno GraphiC. (Clara fired Daisy after an attempt at blackmail; this was DeVoe's revenge.)

The GraphiC's avid readers soon learned just how "devoted" Miss DeVoe had been; she kept tabs on all the gentleman callers to Clara's Chinese Den. The benign Buddha that presided there didn't talk, but Daisy made up for it. The four-year register of Clara's beaux read like a roll-call of he-man talent. In addition to agreeable Doc Pearson, the list ranged from comics (Eddie Cantor) to cowboys (Rex Bell and newcomer Gary Cooper) to heavies (Bela Lugosi). And that wasn't all.

The list, in GraphiC installments, was just a little too long; poor gregarious Clara took on Trojans by the bunch. She'd play party girl to the entire "Thundering Herd" (crack University of Southern California football team) during beery, brawling, gangbanging weekend parties, accommodating the fun-loving bruisers right down to the eleventh man: hulking tackle Marion Morrison (later

← Clara and the cowboy she married: Rex Bell

known as John Wayne).

The Golden Circle decided Clara had gone a <u>little</u> beyond bounds, as her considerable venereal achievements were not just dressing-room gossip, they were reported on page one. The "It" Girl was said to have showered her beloved "Thundering Herd" with gold cigarette cases and cuff links; furnished several Trojan frat houses (which housed her sex-athletes) with bootleg booze and squandered her cash playing all-night poker in the kitchen with her chauffeur, cook, and maid.

Clara took Daisy to the L.A. courts. After a battle royal, with cat fur and lurid charges on both sides, Miss DeVoe was packed off to jail for pilfering large sums from the Bow bank account.

Clara's victory was hollow: all those red-hot headlines hurt. The incandescent redhead had become too hot to handle. She married Rex Bell in an effort to cool things out, but her career hit the skids and

she slid over the edge into the first of a series of nervous breakdowns. Before signing on at the sanitarium she issued a statement: "I've been working hard for years, and I need a rest. So I'm figuring on going to Europe for a year or more, when my contract expires." When her contract expired some months later,

Clara's Fortune ↑   Clara and Rex ↑   "IT" →

sound-mixing engineer in the monitor room, unfamiliar with the Brooklynese boom of Clara's voice, didn't tune down his dials for Clara's greeting.

She made her entrance, hollered "HELLO, EVERYBODY!" — and blew every valve in the recording room.

The eclipse of Clara Bow, who had been for an entire generation Flaming Youth personified, cinched Hollywood's reputation as the Place Where Girls Go Wrong. The public bought it for a fact: Clara just couldn't have learned to carry on like that back in sedate old Brooklyn! The round of clergymen, politicos and purity leagues took up the call once again, with all the furor of the Lynch-Fatty days: another luminary shot down in flames. After Clara had proved herself a Scarlet Woman the Answer Man of the pulpit, Dr. S. Parkes Cadman, adjudged Hollywood with doomsday finality "The Cemetery of Virtue."

oft-burnt Paramount did not renew.

The case of the blowing valves had not helped. Her first talkie, The Wild Party, tried to milk those headlines. Her first scene called for her to dash into a girl's dorm with the line, "Hello, everybody!" The

· SATURN OVER SUNSET ·

The great big golden illusion ripped wide open on Tuesday, October 29, 1929. Variety put it this way:

WALL STREET LAYS AN EGG.

Describing Hollywood's Golden People from a perspective of twenty years, Mae Murray confided: "We were like dragonflies. We seemed to be suspended effortlessly in the air, but in reality, our wings were beating very, very fast . . ."

For many of the Golden People, already shaken by the arrival of the Talkies, this was a final day of reckoning. It was Solon's fateful moment: "But in every matter we must mark well the end; for oftentimes God gives men a gleam of happiness, and then plunges them into ruin."

John Gilbert's debacle was an extreme case. He had been the highest-paid star of 1928, receiving $10,000 a week from MGM ever since he had packed them in with The Big Parade. After his affair with Garbo had fizzled out, Gilbert married Broadway actress Ina Claire on the rebound. He was in mid-Atlantic, returning from a squabbly honeymoon, when the bubble burst.

Gilbert docked in New York to discover he was broke. Like many other Hollywoodians, he had invested in stocks on margin, a victim of one of the investment sharpies who infested the film colony. (He would have done better had he slept on his salary — like Emil Jannings who, during his short Hollywood career, had kept $200,000 in cash stuffed inside his pillow.)

Jack Gilbert still had an "unbreakable" contract at MGM to fall back on, but this was scant solace after his first Talkie — a bit of fluff titled His Glorious Night — was dubbed a "shriekie."

When the film opened at New York's Capitol Theater, his fans tittered embarrassedly as a caricature of his voice piped out of the loudspeakers like a tinny whine. But Jack's light tenor was in truth not bad. The proof is to be found in a brilliant 1932 comedy, Downstairs, written by Gilbert himself, in which his delivery is excellent. The harm had already been done, however, and columnists and fan magazines spread the word that Gilbert was finished. His fine performance in Downstairs encourages one to lend some credence to the rumor that the sound engineers at MGM, at the orders of L.B. Mayer (who at that point wanted to smash Gilbert's career and get rid of him) played havoc with the trebles and deliberately gelded Gilbert's voice.

Jack was a simple fellow who had

← Norma Talmadge and Nemesis: The Demon Mike

John Gilbert, Screen Lover, Is Found Dead

Film Star, 39, Victim of Heart Attack in Home

WED FOUR TIMES

HOLLYWOOD, Calif., Jan. 9. (AP)—John Gilbert, 39, great lover of the screen, died today at his home here from a heart attack. Death of the movie actor was revealed this morning when the fire department was called to his residence in an effort to revive him with an inhalator.

JOHN GILBERT

grown to need the love-fix from his fans. The abrupt end of the affair hit him hard. The kiss-off was his wife. While Ina Claire's snooty star rose in Talkie Heaven due to her impeccable Beacon Hill diction, Gilbert's star fell. Ina did not hesitate to rub salt into his wounds by constantly apprising him of the situation. Jack took to the newly-legal hard stuff with a vengeance, as did another silent star who had "voice" trouble, Marie Prevost. Her romantic looks didn't fit her Bronx honk, and blonde Marie tried to drown her heartbreak in bourbon. Jack and Marie staged a drink-to-death race which Jack "won" in 1936. Marie dragged on until 1937 when her half-eaten corpse was discovered in her seedy apartment on Cahuenga Boulevard. Her dachshund had survived by making mincemeat of his mistress.

Hollywood has always cannibalized itself. The story of Gilbert's fall turned up on the screen in the 1937 A Star Is Born, though the death scene in that film was inspired by the suicide by drowning of yet another despondent Hollywood actor, John Bowers.

It was a day of reckoning for some front-office men as well. Wall Street wasn't alone in indulging in financial finagling. In 1930 William Fox was accused of

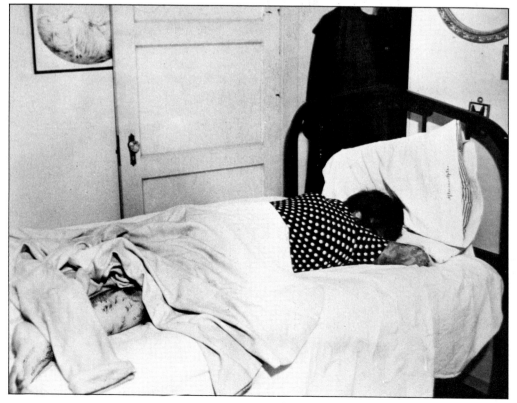

Doggie's Dinner ↑

Marie Prevost →

146

"malfeasance in office, manipulations of assets and misappropriations of funds" and ejected from the splendid studio he had built. Feisty little Adolph Zukor, who had mined a private fortune of $40,000,000 in the Paramount mountain during the Twenties, found himself on the brink of bankruptcy. Even Hearst was in hot water, and this time it was Marion who helped <u>him</u> out.

With the rest of the nation, Hollywood had to face the music — "the greatest, gaudiest spree in history" was over. Many of 1929's one-hundred-million regular moviegoers had switched from theater lines to bread lines. In 1930 attendance was off forty per cent. Some theaters offered desperate come-ons: dish night, 2-for-1 tickets, double features and "free Marcel-wave coupons for the lady patrons." But in the grim dawn of the Great Depression, gimmicks weren't enough to lure back the faithful. Too many factories were closed.

Ads sponsored by the All-Year Club of Southern California appeared in the national magazines: "Come to California for a glorious vacation.

Advise anyone not to come seeking employment, lest he be disappointed; but for tourists the attractions are unlimited."

Hollywood, though shaken by Talkies and the Crash, took stock and pulled through. In the process, the Movieland Mythos took a drubbing. The star system survived (MGM

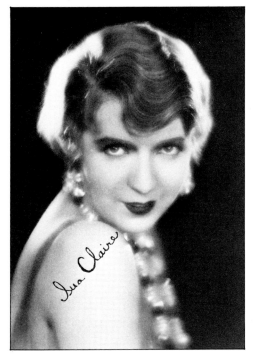

was brutal. Louise Brooks, one of the loveliest visions ever to grace a screen, went from stardom to a Macy's counter in a vertiginous fall from glory. A worse fate than a Macy's counter befell others. Mae Murray, the de luxe millionairess Princess Mdivani, was shed by her doubtfully noble spouse when she lost her fortune. After a period of misfortune she was arrested for vagrancy when discovered one night sleeping on a bench in Central Park.

The great luminaries of the Twenties, like Mae Murray, truly believed in their stardom as a Divine Right. Mae was not the only one who sought to elevate herself above ordinary mortals by marrying a title. Gloria Swanson became the Marquise de la Falaise de Coudray; Pola Negri (née Apolonia Chalupec) traded her Countess Dombska title for Princess, marrying the last available Mdivani, Prince Serge. A few years later she was ditched by Prince, Paramount and popularity.

launched the motto "More Stars Than There Are In Heaven") though the stars themselves could only wonder how long they would stay in their orbits.

Twenty-six new Talkie stars had appeared by 1931; only three remained from the stellar roster of 1921. Gilbert's was not the only career on the skids. His comrades in dismay were Conrad Nagel, Charles Farrell, Buddy Rogers and William Haines. Ramon Novarro, ever dramatic, "retired" to a monastery for a spell.

The going was equally rough for silent goddesses: Billie Dove, Colleen Moore, Corinne Griffith and Norma Talmadge waned. Some, like Talmadge, pretended to be "too rich to care."

For some beauties the eclipse

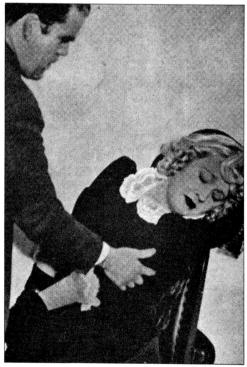

Louise Brooks ↑   Mae Murray arrested for vagrancy ↑   Princess Mdivani takes aim →

· DRASTIC DOUBTS ·

William Blake put it well: "If a star should doubt, it would immediately go out." With the Crash, this happened in Hollywood. In spades.

The strain proved too much for many former Greats. Rather than live among the rubble, these chose to Make an End. Some made dramatic tableaux of their suicides — gods self-slain on their own strange altars. It was at this period that the expression "has-been" was first coined. It was a label hard to shake, however unfairly it had been stuck on.

Some of the "Lucky Stars" who managed to march through the twin holocaust of the Talkies/Crash unscathed, made a show of pointedly ignoring the grimmer realities. Such a Lucky Star was gutsy jazz baby Joan Crawford.

In 1932, in the depths of the Depression, Crawford felt called upon to fortify the nation's morale with a publicity manifesto in Photoplay titled "Spend!" — a defiant declaration of rights of the star.

In answer to a groundswell of grumbles across the country that movie stars were grossly overpaid, Joan replied it was the star's duty to maintain the style of living the public associates with her exalted station. With iron determination, she must surround herself with the height of luxury, fashionable furs, dazzling jewelry, an ever-replenished wardrobe of fabulous creations. This way, and this way only, the fans will be satisfied and dollars will stay in circulation.

Bravely, Joan exhorted her fans to imitate her: "I, Joan Crawford, I Believe in the Dollar. Everything I Earn, I Spend!"

For Joan, at least, it was the religious perpetuation of the Hollywood Way of Life — magnificent mansions, motorcars, cascades of luxuries, life outside the studios a whirl of cocktail parties, well-publicized night-club dates, romantic rendezvous.

She played it to the hilt. She, like the others, had stared over the brink, and Oblivion had stared right back up. Joan knew where she came from and did not want to go back there.

The Crash punctured Hollywood's brassy self-confidence. In the still night of their gilded souls, the surviving stars — Crawford among them — knew something alien had crawled up on their privileged plateau: a rat named Angst.

Scandal made its entrance in 1930 with the wild court battle featuring Clara Bow vs. Daisy DeVoe. But the show played to a half-empty house.

← Joan Crawford: Faith in Herself

Buster Keaton: Desolation Row →

Even with Clara's romances spelled out in the tabloids, the nation was too dazed to be very concerned. The Clara Affair was an unwelcome backward glance at a binge that had given everyone a hangover.

In 1931, when Clara suffered her first nervous breakdown, many of her former fans were out looking for jobs. While Clara recovered in a rest home, a multitude faced a harsher music than jazz. Though Clara's Talkie comeback the following year was brilliant, Call Her Savage did not save the day. Clara was a relic and the pain of it drove her insane. Back to the sanitarium, cooled down in ice-watered sheets.

Soon to join Clara in the sanitarium was Buster Keaton, who was unhinged by the combined traumas of the arrival of sound, loss of artistic control of his films, marital problems and drink.

Buster Keaton: Genius unhinged ↑   Daisy DeVoe (center) ↑   Clara in court: Betrayed by Daisy →

158

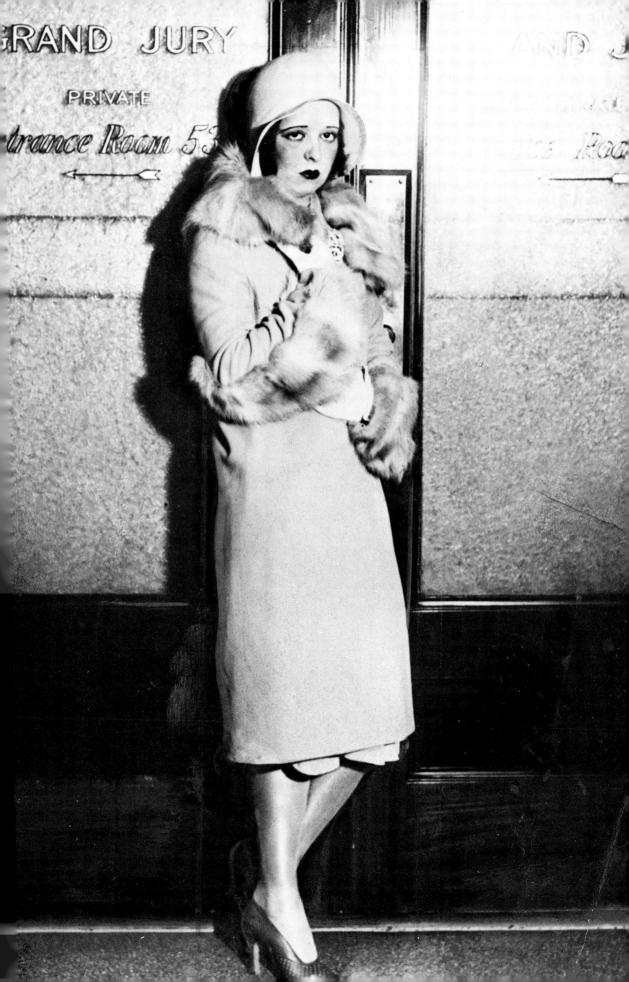

· ENDITALLS ·

The stars whose jangled nerves led to private mental homes, such as Clara Bow and Buster Keaton, made less noise in falling than those who wrote their own fade-out. Rather than face life anywhere else than on the summit, Milton Sills chose to write <u>Finis</u> in 1930 by hurtling his last limousine over Dead Man's Curve on Sunset Boulevard. The brilliant actress, Jeanne Eagels, opted for a deliberate overdose of heroin. Robert Ames took the gas pipe in 1931. Karl Dane put a revolver to his temple in 1932.

Hollywood's Father Confessor also shot himself in 1932, becoming the decade's most talked-about suicide. His compassionate nature had earned Paul Bern the title, and may well have been one of Jean Harlow's reasons for marrying this physically unprepossessing intellectual, twenty-two years her senior. He was Thalberg's assistant at MGM and had been instrumental in bringing Jean to the Culver City factory.

The odd couple was married on July 2, 1932. Two months later, on September 5, 1932, the butler found Bern's body in his wife's all-white bedroom in their Benedict Canyon mansion. He was nude, sprawled in front of a full-length mirror, drenched in Jean's favorite perfume, Mitsouko, shot through the head by a .38 pistol which lay by his side. Jean was visiting her mother at the time.

The butler did not notify the police but phoned MGM instead. Soon Louis B. Mayer and Thalberg were on the scene. Mayer found a note in Bern's handwriting on top of Jean's vanity table:

Dearest Dear,
Unfortunately this is the only way to make good the frightful wrong I have done you, and to wipe out my abject humiliation. I Love you.
Paul
You understand that last night was only a comedy.

It seems Bern had a "problem" and that he had tried to effect intercourse by artificial means: a realistic phony phallus. Mayer pocketed this note and when the police finally arrived two and a half hours later, only turned it over when the studio publicist, Howard Strickling, insisted he do so.

The following day, Dorothy Millette, a blonde would-be starlet who had been Paul Bern's first wife, drowned herself in the Sacramento River.

← Paul Bern's body in Harlow's bedroom

Two has-been actors turned alcoholics drowned themselves. John Bowers walked nude into the waves at Malibu; James Murray jumped clothed into the East River. George Hill, talented director of The Big House, blew his head off with a hunting rifle in 1934.

Lou Tellegen's suicide in 1935 was not unique: his hideous hara-kiri with a pair of gold scissors imitated that of Max Linder, ten years earlier. Those scissors, engraved with Tellegen's name, had been busy in former years cutting out press items covering his screen career as Geraldine Farrar's leading man and their well-publicized romance and marriage. Completely forgotten by 1935, Lou surrounded himself with the fat scrapbooks of yellowing

Dearest Dear,
unfortunately this is the only way to make good the frightful wrong I have done you and to wipe out my abject humiliation, I love you.
Paul
You understand that last night it was only a comedy

Members of the wedding: Thalberg, Harlow, Shearer and Bern →

newspaper clippings of his days of glory, laid out all his most flattering photos, with tattered posters of his triumphs, The Long Trail and The Redeeming Sin. Nude in the center of this mocking circle he squatted Japanese-style and began belaboring the has-been he had become with ferocious scissors stabs to his belly and chest. Lou was found eviscerated, heart laid bare, his pathetic souvenirs drenched in blood.

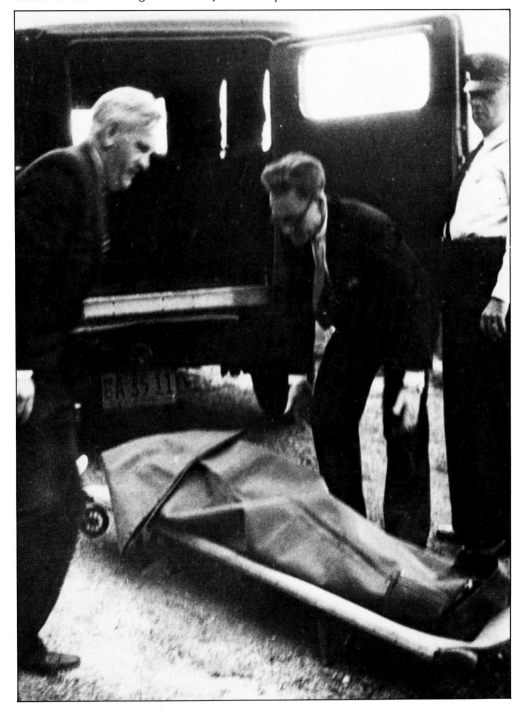

Bern's body is removed from Benedict Canyon ↑

Newspaper clippings also played a part in the suicide of exquisite Gwili Andre, a model and failed starlet who had garnered many inches of press coverage but few feet of celluloid. Gwili was found burnt to a crisp in a funeral pyre of her useless publicity.

A trend was started by Peg Entwistle, who climbed the steep slopes of Mount Lee to the Hollywood Sign, which in the Thirties spelt out in giant letters the name of Mack Sennett's ill-fated real estate venture, HOLLYWOODLAND, and clambered to the top of the thirteenth letter (Peg had a bit in Thirteen Women, but it led to no other offers.) She could not go on facing indifferent Tinsel Town. Peg dove to her death. Other disillusioned starlets followed her lead, and the Hollywood Sign became a notorious signing-off place.

Seconal sleeping pills proved popular, and took away Warner's charmer Ross Alexander in 1937 and director Tom Forman in 1938.

Gwili Andre: Flaming Finale ↑   Jumping-off place ↑   Peg Entwistle: Sky Diver →

· BABYLON BABBLERS ·

Aside from those scandals which made the papers, Hollywood has always had its own supply of inner-sanctum scandal tales, prattle that livened the boredom between takes, but never saw the light of a gossip column. Depression insecurity brought out the worst in the Bitch Goddess: stars struck out at stars, directors inveighed against directors, front-office men trashed everyone in sight.

The calumny mill worked overtime at such niteries as the Trocadero, the Cocoanut Grove, Casanova, Cotton Club, Hawaiian Paradise, Club Marti, Bali, Club Esquire, Century Club, and the Famous Door. Forked tongues wagged at such favored bars as the Beachcombers, Seven Seas, Tropics, Bamboo Room, Swing Club, and the Cinebar. Gay gossip swirled at Mary's, the dike bar of the Strip, and its opposite number up the hill, Café Gala, home away from home for Cole Porter and Cecil Beaton. Reputations were devoured along with dinner at the Brown Derby, Cock and Bull, Avdeef's, La Golondrina, Victor Hugo, Dave Chasen's, Cinegrill, Biltmore, Gotham, Musso-Frank's and La Maze. At these Banquets of Reputations, all Hollywood was fair game.

Those "items" where public image and private life were wildly at odds were the favorites, like the famous love team of Charlie Farrell and Janet Gaynor, where she was more butch than he. Marriages such as Farrell's to Virginia Valli or Gaynor's to Adrian were referred to as Twilight Tandems, lavender cover-ups.

Catty talk also focussed on anything private and slightly singular, such as the sadistic streak of Stroheim, Selznick, Victor McLaglen or Wally Beery, or the masochistic needs of Jannings, Laughton, or the mad, gorgeous Mary Nolan, known as la belle masochiste. (Mary was the notorious ex-Imogene Wilson, Ziegfeld Girl whose SM psychodramas with comic Frank Tinney had scandalized New York.) In Hollywood as in Gotham, Mary brought out the sadist in men, often to the point where she could exact the M's Revenge, as when she sued a producer in 1935 for $500,000 for roughing her up too well.

Organ talk was similarly popular. Chaplin and Bogart led the list of the well-endowed; equal time was devoted to those who did not measure up. The names of those love goddesses were bandied about whose devotion to Priapus required having their cunts surgically "taken in."

The wicked wit of a Lombard or a Bankhead transformed such dishery into drollery.

Homosexuality, real or supposed, was a favorite topic. Few around the Fox lot had not heard that director F.W. Murnau favored gays when it came to casting. Murnau's death in 1931 inspired a flood tide of speculation.

Murnau had hired as valet a handsome fourteen-year-old Filipino boy named Garcia Stevenson. The boy was at the wheel of the Packard when the fatal accident occurred. The Hollywood _méchantes langues_ reported that Murnau was going down on Garcia when the car leaped off the road. Only eleven brave souls (Garbo was there) showed up for the funeral. Farrell and Gaynor, who

had been directed by Murnau in three great films, did not pay their respects. Garbo commissioned a death mask of Murnau and the solitary Swede kept this memento of the German genius on her desk during all of her years in Hollywood.

Garbo's genuine reserve held

the gossips at bay for the most part. There was, however, occasional speculation about how close her friendship really was with writer Salka Viertel.

Further fodder was provided by the arrival of Marlene Dietrich. By all accounts a joyous bisexual with an appetite for many loves, Marlene

Charlie Farrell and Janet Gaynor

Murnau: German genius →

GOSSIP, HIDDEN CHAN

GOSSIP, said George Eliot, "proves nothing but the bad taste" of the gossiper, a truth which errs only on the side of understatement.

Gossip can be in bad taste, and much more and **WORSE**.

It can be thoughtless and inconsiderate.

And it can also be malicious and **CRUEL**.

Innocence can be pilloried by gossip, repentance frustrated, evil itself compounded beyond all limits of reason or justice.

The first and **BEST** of the three ancient admonitions against gossip is:

"Speak no evil!"

The other two, as we all remember, are to neither **HEAR** nor **SEE** evil.

They make a good rule, if applied with wisdom.

It is not wise, of course, to let silence, blindness or deafness to evil things constitute a license **FOR** evil things.

Wickedness, corruption, inhumanities are evils which neither wise, virtuous nor practical men contend against with silent tongues, deaf ears or closed eyes.

To **RECOGNIZE** evil is to be armed with **TRUTH**, and the cour-age to **TELL** the truth and **HEAR** the truth is essential to triumph over evil.

So ancient philosophy very probably intended no license or comfort for evil things or evil-doers.

More probably it intended admonition against the futherance of evil through cruel reflection upon atoned deeds or untrue distortions of facts.

In other words, **GOSSIP**—malicious repetition of things better left unsaid or **NEVER TRUE**.

Gossip is a rolling stone that **DOES** gather moss.

It grows like a
the nose of Pinnoc
had a **BIGGER** no
As Alexander I

"The flying run
Scarce any tale
And all who tol
And all who hea

It is no defens
TENDS no harm.

EL OF MALICIOUS EVIL

TRUTH that inevitably attaches to the rolling stone of gossip and rumor.

A careless tongue speculates upon what **MIGHT** be.

A careless ear misses the element of **IMAGINING**, falsely translates and repeats it as **FACT**.

And perhaps a priceless reputation is irreparably ruined, a precious character irretrievably lost.

The obligation to **WEIGH THE TRUTH** of what is seen, heard and spoken cannot rest lightly upon any honest man.

Falsehoods fed into the minds of the people serve the **CORRUPT ENDS** of the enemies of the people.

Propagandists, able to set idle tongues wagging, are given the power to ruin innocent lives, wreck industries, communities, even nations.

Gossip is the hidden channel through which hate, suspicion and intolerance, causes of most of the world's distress and many of its wars, enter the minds of people **CARELESS OF TRUTH**.

You must **KNOW THE TRUTH** of what you see and hear to know that what you **SAY** is true.

lling down hill, like r every lie he told

as they rolled, ard than told; mething new, argements, too."

ssiper that he **IN-** nly passes the false

tale along as it comes to him, he perpetuates the cruelty.

Nearly always the gossiper defends himself with the excuse that he did not **START** the story.

What does it matter where the origin of a cruel deed has been, if **WE** are cruel and not merciful or forgiving?

In truth, the origin of gossip usually borders on the innocent and the innocuous.

The malice it gathers is the moss of UN-

CARY GRANT in who's a fairy?

kept the magpies chirping right
through the Thirties. Her passel of
girlfriends was dubbed "Marlene's
Sewing Circle." They were not
lesbians, like Nazimova's gang, but
good-time Charlenes who, like
Marlene, swung both ways. Marlene
was ascribed a passionate affair
with fellow Paramount star, Claudette
Colbert, as well as one with Lili
Damita. The vision of Marlene in a
man's tuxedo proved irresistible
to certain members of the international
set: authoress Mercedes d'Acosta
and millionairess Jo Carstairs, both of
whom were very much at home
in masculine attire themselves. They
made pilgrimages to Hollywood
to pay their respects to "The Blue
Angel." It was in 1932, while her
Sewing Circle was forming, that Marlene
started wearing "man drag" off
screen; a nationwide vogue, women-in-
slacks, was launched.

The ambisex allure of Marlene in
"man drag" was magnified by
her Svengali, Josef von Sternberg,
who managed to include a scene
of her dressed as a man in each of the
films they made together. That
their affair was a romance of the head,
of art and artifice, there is no
doubt. Sternberg's Marlene fetish did

← Lili Damita: AC-DC   Cary Grant "honored" in a Tijuana Bible ↑   Man-drag for Marlene ↑

not meet with universal approbation. Vanity Fair commented after The Scarlet Empress: "Sternberg traded his open style for fancy play, chiefly upon the legs in silk, and buttocks in lace, of Dietrich, of whom he has made a paramount slut. By his own token, Sternberg is a man of meditation as well as a man of action: but instead of contemplating the navel of Buddha, his umbilical perseverance is fixed on the navel of Venus." Mrs. von Sternberg (Risa Royce) also disapproved, and filed for divorce, naming Marlene as responsible for "alienating the affections of my husband."

Marlene went on to become a legend, with other lovers, male and female, other directors, other cameramen. In later days, when one of the latter proved incapable of lighting her properly, the quasi-eternal glamor girl was heard muttering, "Where are you, Joe?"

← Table talk: Clara Bow eavesdrops   Sternberg: Prisoner of his obsession ↑

·MONSTER MAE·

Mae West rode into Hollywood with a reputation as the Bad Girl of Broadway for plays like Sex, which got her into hot water and eight days of jail. On arrival in 1932 she quipped, "I'm not a little girl from a little town makin' good in a big town. I'm a big girl from a big town makin' good in a little town."

Paramount's move in signing Mae was a gamble that paid off. She stole the picture with a supporting role in Night After Night and thereafter wrangled the studio bosses into allowing her to run her own show. Her first starring film, She Done Him Wrong, which she adapted from her own play Diamond Lil, broke box-office records for 1933. It took in $2,000,000 in three months and saved the studio from bankruptcy.

Variety summed up the film: "Miss West in picture hats, straight-jacket gowns and with so much jewelry she looks like a Knickerbocker ice plant, sings 'Easy Rider,' 'A Guy What Takes His Time,' and 'Frankie and Johnny.' All somewhat cleaned up lyrically — but Mae couldn't sing a lullaby without making it sexy . . . As full of laughs as an agent is of alibis, the entire production depends on the personality of the 'Sex' star who gets across each jibe and point with a delivery that will soon be imitated

. . . Her handling of lovers, past, present and prospective comprises the whole picture."

Mae didn't knock all Hollywood dead. A notable resister was Mary Pickford, who commented from her retreat at Pickfair: "I passed the door of my young niece's room — she's been raised, oh, so carefully — and I heard her singing bits from that song from Diamond Lil — I say 'that song' just because I'd blush to quote the title even here."

Stronger disapprobation of Mae's fun-loving views on sex came spewing forth from Cardinal Mundelein of Chicago. The Cardinal ordered one of his professional prigs, the Jesuit Rev. Daniel A. Lord, to pen a pamphlet, "The Motion Pictures Betray America," in which Catholic youth was urged to boycott the "obnoxious pictures" of Mae West. All of them would henceforth be blacklisted in Father Lord's magazine, The Queen's Work.

The Catholic sodality were so gratified at the response that they decided to put their anti-sex boycott on a national level. Bernard J. Sheil, auxiliary bishop of Chicago, set about organizing a pressure group: the National Legion of Decency was formed in October 1933, six months after the release of

← Mae: Already a Star

She Done Him Wrong. The Legion heavies cited the menace Mae West represented as one of the major reasons for the "necessity" of their organization.

Mae followed She Done Him Wrong with her most successful picture, I'm No Angel. The clamp down began with her third feature, It Ain't No Sin. When huge posters advertising It Ain't No Sin were up on Broadway, a squad of priests marched up and down in front of the ads, with signs bearing this succint message: "IT IS." The Decent Legionnaires won a minor victory; the title was changed to Belle of the Nineties. The Paramount publicist who had been working on a zany promotion stunt was stuck with fifty parrots who had been cued to repeat "It Ain't No Sin" over and over again.

By this time Father Lord had taken his busy body to Hollywood where he went about teaching Hays a thing or two about censorship. Lord dusted off Hays's old list of "Don'ts" and with the help of a lay Catholic, Martin Quigley, wrote a new set of ridiculous restrictions under the title "A Code to Govern the Making of Motion and Talking Pictures." This monstrosity included 100 different ways to de-ball the movies. Hays was handed these even stiffer moral fibers by Lord and Quigley, and Joseph I. Breen was installed to enforce the Code with a new weapon — the Purity Seal. A picture could not be exhibited without it.

Mae's war with the super-censors started in earnest the summer of 1934, when the new guardians of America's virtue pounced on her way of handling a gangster: "Is that a gun in your pocket, or are you just glad to see me?"

While It Ain't No Sin was in production, the Hays Office had

GRAND J
Witnesses (
Entrance

· DIARY IN BLUE ·

The Thirties was endowed with another lady luminary with a pronounced penchant for men, an auburn-haired beauty, poised sophisticate with a sensuous throaty voice: Mary Astor, one of the screen's great character actresses.

Since girlhood, Mary's best friend and confidante had been her diary. She told it everything, and delighted in setting down a sublime experience while the memory still glowed. She could relive the moment and mark the high spots of her passage through life. Her Hollywood Diary was bound in blue, its pages covered with fine, ultrafeminine, flowing script that graphologists have affirmed is remarkably free from inhibitions. Its contents were as free as her penmanship. The volume for 1935 covered her extramarital trysts with witty playwright George S. Kaufman, with whom she found exquisite rapport; it is odd she didn't keep it well hidden.

The blue book had been kept tossed in a bedroom drawer, in with Mary's undies. One day, her physician husband was hunting a pair of misplaced cufflinks. When Dr. Franklyn Thorpe idly opened the leather volume, his glance fell on a passage of extravagant admiration: ". . . remarkable staying power. I don't

see how he does it!" The admiration was not for Dr. Thorpe.

As Dr. Thorpe turned the pages, he learned that the man with such fantastic staying power was the urbane Kaufman, man-about-New York. He and Mary had met at the Algonquin during a New York shopping spree she had indulged in during the summer of 1933. This meant the good doctor had been a good cuckold for a good sixteen months. Mary recorded her first encounter with her paramour-to-be (introduced by friend Miriam Hopkins) in glowing terms:
His first initial is G. — George Kaufman — and I fell like a ton of bricks. I met him Friday . . . Saturday he called for me at the Ambassador and we went to the Casino for lunch and had a very gay time!

After taking in a performance of Kaufman's Of Thee I Sing at the Music Box Theatre, Mary and George did the town for the next few nights — clubs, dives, penthouse parties. The disillusioned doctor's eyes popped as he read his wife's own record of her sexual itinerary: Monday — we ducked out of the boring party . . . it was very hot so we got a cab and drove around the park a few times and the park was, well,

← Mary Astor on the witness stand: Her most dramatic role

the park, and he held my hand and said he'd like to kiss me but didn't . . .

Tuesday night we had a dinner at Twenty-One and on the way to see <u>Run Little Chillun</u> he did kiss me — and I don't think either of us remember much what the show was about. We played kneesies during the first two acts, my hand wasn't in my own lap during the third . . . It's been years since I've felt up a man in public, but I just got carried away . . .

Afterwards we had a drink someplace and then went to a little flat in 73rd Street where we could be alone, and it was all very thrilling and beautiful. Once George lays down his glasses, he is <u>quite</u> a different man. His powers of recuperation are amazing, and we made love all night long . . . It all worked perfectly, and we shared our fourth climax at dawn . . .

I didn't see much of anybody else the rest of the time — we saw every show in town, had grand fun together and went frequently to 73rd Street where he fucked the living daylights out of me . . .

One morning about 4 we had a sandwich at Reuben's, and it was just getting daylight, so we drove through the park in an open cab, and the birds started singing, and it was a cool and dewy day and it was pretty heavenly to pet and French . . . right out in the open . . .

Was any woman every happier? It seems that George is just hard all the time . . . I don't see how he does it, he is perfect.

Dr. Thorpe then discovered that the heady New York affair had continued right near his own back yard.

Mary Astor: "Was any woman ever happier?" ↑

Kaufman and Moss Hart passed a few days in Hollywood in February 1934 before setting up their winter writing headquarters in Palm Springs. One morning, when Mary told Thorpe she was going to Warner's for a costume fitting, she raced instead to Kaufman's hotel: Monday I went to the Beverly Wilshire and was able to see George alone for the first time. He greeted me in pajamas, and we flew into each other's arms. He was rampant in an instant, and in a few moments it was just like old times . . . he tore out of his pajamas and I never was undressed by anyone so fast in all my life . . . Later we went to Vendome for lunch, to a stationer's shop . . . then back to the hotel. It was raining and lovely. It was wonderful to fuck the entire sweet afternoon away . . . I left about 6 o'clock.

On subsequent weekends in Palm Springs:
Sat around in the sun all day — lunch in the pool with Moss and George and the Rogers — dinner at the Dunes — a drink in the moonlight WITHOUT Moss and Rogers. Ah, desert night — with George's body plunging into mine, naked under the stars . . .

When Thorpe confronted his wife with his discovery, one might

suppose the blue-bound book would go blank for a spell. But Mary couldn't wait to record her husband's reaction:

He was very badly broken up for several days, used his final weapon with me, "I need you," with tears.

For the sake of peace and respite from all this emotionalism, I told him I would do nothing at the present. My main reason for saying that is, quite honestly, I want to be able to see George for the rest of his stay here without being all upset — looking like hell. I want to have the last few times of completely enjoying him . . .

Mary's refusal to break off the affair caused Thorpe to retaliate; soon, he was being seen with so many starlets that his digressions became the talk of the town. When Thorpe sued Mary for divorce in April 1935, and demanded the custody of their daughter Marilyn (adored by Mary), hundreds of eyebrows were raised.

Mary did not contest the divorce. Thorpe had appropriated her tell-all Diary before she moved out of their Beverly Hills mansion. It was devastating evidence. She could not face the prospect of being deprived of her daughter. She filed a counter-suit on July 15, to retain custody of the child.

Thorpe's lawyers revealed the existence of the Diary the first day of the trial. The judge, "Goody" Knight, took a peek at the book and excluded it as evidence. But Thorpe's lawyers leaked excerpts to the press which left little doubt as to its tenor; among them was the "Ah, desert night . . ." passage which quickly entered into folklore. The tabloids gave the Diary full coverage, long excerpts sprinkled with asterisks. The public had a ball filling in the dots for itself.

Older fans recalled another of Mary Astor's passionate affaires de coeur, a decade earlier before her marriage, when as a budding film star (during the making of Don Juan) she had been John Barrymore's young mistress.

The court got an earful when the nurse of Mary's daughter related what had been going on chez Thorpe after Madame Thorpe moved out. The nurse described a scene with starlet Norma Taylor who got into a jealous brawl with Thorpe in front of the child. At the time Norma had on red toenail polish and nothing else. Nurse reported that not only Norma, but three other blonde Busby Berkeley showgirls had "slept in the doctor's bed" on succeeding nights. And Thorpe's wereabouts? Her deadpan reply was: "He was right there in his bed too!"

Mary got back mansion and Marilyn, in spite of all the Diary revealed of her passion for Kaufman. However, the court did not return her Dearest Friend. The diary was adjudged "pornography" and consigned to the courthouse stove.

It is significant that these revelations did not injure Mary Astor's career — far from it. Ten years earlier, a case like this would have finished off any star, but the Depression had been a factor, albeit painful, in promoting greater public maturity. In a few years, Mary would score one of her greatest successes as the seductive villainess in The Maltese Falcon.

Kaufman had taken a powder during the courtroom proceedings; he sat them out in New York with Hart. He dodged queries concerning the case, but once, when cornered by reporters at the stage door of the Music Box, he allowed: "You may say I did not keep a diary."

Mary got Marilyn →

·DEATH GARAGE·

1935, the year that Mary Astor's explosive Diary was incinerated, ended with a sickening thud — one of Hollywood's most mystifying murders. Solved crimes are generally filed and forgotten; the unsolved leave a lingering malaise which refuses to disappear. This happened with the case of the Ice Cream Blonde.

Delectable Thelma Todd worked with Laurel and Hardy, the Marx Brothers and her friend Zasu Pitts in a series of riotous farces for Hal Roach. Her fans would not have recognized Thelma in her final role — one that was only played after a struggle — that of a slumped corpse, her mouth, evening gown and mink coat spotted with blood. Her maid discovered the body at 10:30 Monday morning, December 16, on opening the door of the garage Thelma shared with her lover, director Roland West. The garage was on the Palisades, above the Pacific Highway, between Santa Monica and Malibu. The ignition switch of her open Packard convertible was turned on, the motor dead, with Thelma slumped in the front seat. By a macabre coincidence, she had once played a scene with Groucho Marx in which he had warned her, "Now be a good girlie, or I'll lock you up in the garage."

The Grand Jury, after weeks of puzzling over contradictory evidence, handed in an odd verdict: "Death due to carbon monoxide poisoning." This perfunctory verdict left much unexplained. If she had died from asphyxiation, how did Thelma's clothing get into such a state of rumpled disarray? Who or what had caused the blood on her face?

If she had died Sunday morning after returning from the Trocadero, as the police affirmed, what of the witnesses (one of them was West's wife, Jewel Carmen) who claimed to have seen Thelma Sunday morning, whizzing past the intersection of Hollywood and Vine at the wheel of her Packard convertible, with a dark and handsome unidentified man at her side?

Thelma had been West's mistress for some time. They co-managed Thelma Todd's Roadside Rest, a popular beach café nestled under the Palisades on the Coast Highway near the scene of the crime. After lengthy questioning, West reluctantly admitted to a violent quarrel with Thelma during that Sunday's wee hours. He had cut it short by pushing her outside. Neighbors reported hearing Thelma screaming obscenities at West and pounding on the massive hacienda-style door

---

← Thelma Todd: Ice-Cream Blonde

Thelma: Her final role →

to Thelma, money that was swallowed up by the complicated finances of the Roadside Rest, and never repaid to Zasu. Ida Lupino testified that although Thelma seemed as carefree as usual at the Trocadero party, she revealed that she was cheating on West and having a dynamite affair with a businessman in San Francisco.

Thelma's lawyer demanded a second inquest which he said would bolster his theory: she had been murdered by hit-men working for Lucky Luciano. Luciano was then making inroads into illicit California gambling establishments. He had approached Thelma with an offer to take over the upper storey of her café for the installation of a secret and crooked casino which she was supposed to populate with fashionable customers from among her famous friends. The lawyer was convinced that in turning down Luciano's offer, Thelma had signed her

with her fists. An examination of the front door did reveal fresh kick marks.

It was brought out at the inquest that her bosom pal and screen partner, Zasu Pitts, had lent thousands of dollars

Zasu Pitts: Thelma's generous friend →

death warrant. Producer Hal
Roach turned grey at the mere mention
of Luciano's name. He prevailed
upon the attorney to let the matter drop.

It was also suspected, but never
proven, that some sort of staged event
had taken place, arranged by West,
aided by a girl friend who was made to
pass for Thelma. The stand-in is
said to have gone through the scream
and kick routine on West's
doorstep, while behind the door West
knocked Thelma out, placed her
in the car, turned on the ignition and
closed the door of the garage.
According to this theory, West had
wanted to break off their deteriorated
relationship for some time, and
to commit, as in his film Alibi, the
perfect crime. Real proof along
these lines did not come forth, but
West (who had directed Lon

Chaney in The Monster and Chester
Morris in The Bat Whispers, one
of the most extraordinary thrillers
ever filmed) never made another
picture. He married Lola Lane and
died in obscurity in 1952.

Thelma had been popular with fans
and film folk alike. Her funeral at
Forest Lawn pulled in a large crowd.
She lay in an open casket,
blanketed in yellow roses, and thanks
to the Lawn's technicians she
once again resembled the delicate
Ice Cream Blonde with a heart
of gold and a flip remark on her lips.
Zasu Pitts noted: "Why Thelma
looked as if she was going to sit up
and talk." Thelma was through
with talking though, not even a sentence
to tell who had bumped her off. Her
murder will remain one of Hollywood's
most vexing enigmas.

Thelma's funeral at Forest Lawn ↑

· IN LIKE FLYNN ·

The tone of Hollywood scandals changed when, in 1942, Errol Flynn was charged with statutory rape. Peggy Satterlee and Betty Hansen, the girls involved, were under eighteen. One claimed to be raped by land, one by sea.

Charming, easygoing Flynn had been one of Hollywood's best-liked figures, off and on screen, ever since his swashbuckling image had been fixed as "Captain Blood." He was born in Tasmania, and after a rowdy boyhood during which he was thrown out of many schools there and in Australia, made a strong impression as Fletcher Christian in The Wake of the Bounty — the first Bounty film. After several unremarkable roles in England and Hollywood, he hit the jackpot with Captain Blood, and went on to become one of Warners' top stars in such films as The Adventures of Robin Hood. He became an idol of the young in movies which were obviously fun to make and even more fun to watch, and which usually included the rescue of a pretty girl (most often Olivia de Havilland) at the end of a long pointed sword.

Women of all shapes and ages could not resist running after magnetic Errol. His stormy marriage to sultry, bisexual Lili Damita came to an end in 1942. One evening that year, a rather comic scene was enacted in the living room of Flynn's Mulholland Drive home. A police officer had come to inform the swashbuckler (who could have balled nearly any chick who tickled his fancy) that he was charged with statutory rape. Flynn claimed he didn't even know that there was such an animal. It was explained to him that a California law forbade carnal knowledge of anyone under eighteen, even with their consent; getting seduced by an underage chick could cost you five years in the jug.

The cops had picked up Betty Hansen, a young girl, for vagrancy. Among many interesting items in her possession were the phone numbers of Flynn and his pal Bruce Cabot (who had saved Fay Wray from King Kong). Betty claimed that a tennis match with the guys had been followed by a swim-and-sex party. She said Flynn had undressed, but had kept his socks on throughout.

Flynn denied the accusation, admitted to having seen Betty at a party — nothing more. He was booked and released on bail. On returning home, the actor's phone rang. An unknown voice said: "Tell Jack I want $10,000," and hung up. The entire affair might have been dropped

then and there, if Jack Warner, Flynn's boss, had returned the extortionist's call.

The D.A. did not seem to have a case, but for reasons best known to himself, would not let Flynn go peaceably about his career, which at that point involved personifying one of America's great sports heroes, "Gentleman Jim." The fuzz then dragged in a dancer from The Florentine Gardens, Peggy Satterlee. She was well known around town, but because of her obvious experience and mammoth knockers, no one suspected that this minor tootsie was anything but a major pro. Peggy claimed that Errol had taken her aboard his yacht, the Sirocco, in 1941, and had balled her in front of every porthole.

Headlines (not only in the States, but around the world) proclaimed: ROBIN HOOD CHARGED WITH RAPE. The fans nearly rioted when Flynn arrived to face the Grand Jury. But what had promised to

be a feature-length, courtroom sex drama turned out to be a one-reel farce. In Rashomon fashion, Betty, Peggy and Errol each told a different version of the facts. The jury went out and came back with a quick vindication of Flynn.

It seemed that the affair was closed. Flynn went home, opened a case of champagne and friends and well-wishers came by to celebrate. The studio breathed a sigh of relief — Jim was still a Gentleman!

Then, to everyone's amazement, the District Attorney's office, in a rarely used procedure, overrode the decision of the grand jury and decided to prosecute the star in spite of his acquittal. The studio brought in Jerry Geisler, considered Hollywood's shrewdest attorney, to defend Flynn.

Geisler wisely advised Flynn to prepare for a long trial. The best defense was attack, and even if long-drawn out proceedings would prove a nuisance (as the trial progressed the expression "In Like Flynn" became a GI codeword, which amused more than annoyed its namesake), it would give Geisler time to shatter the girls' credibility by raking up everything that could be found about their tacky pasts — and there was plenty to rake.

Peggy went into great detail about what was supposed to have gone on aboard the Sirocco, but in doing so she overreached herself, and Geisler was able to pick her version of the facts apart. (And why had she waited a whole year to discover she had been raped?) The judge had to bring the court to order when she recounted Flynn's whispering in her ear: "That moon would look more beautiful through a porthole."

When Betty Hansen took the stand and testified that Flynn had taken off her clothes, Geisler charged like the cavalry. First, he got her to admit

Lili Damita: Bisexual wife ↑   Errol as Gentleman Jim →

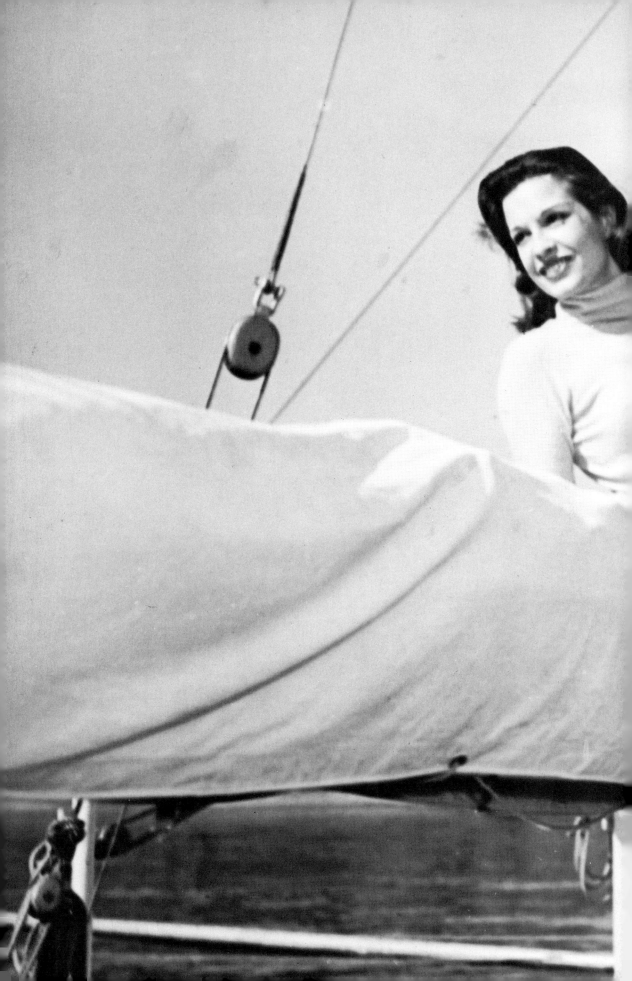

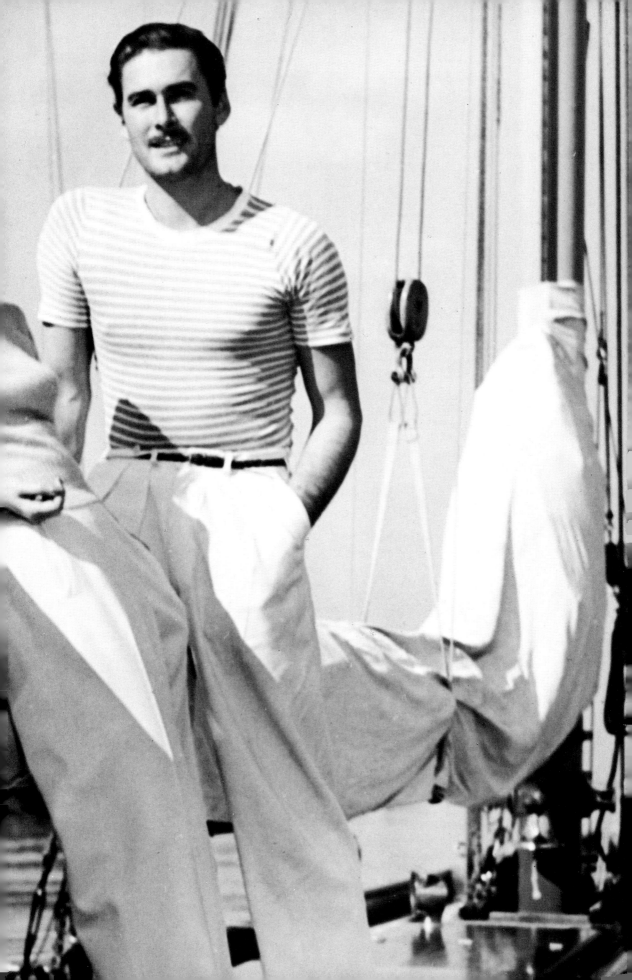

that she had permitted the disrobing, then he thundered at her: "Didn't you want him to take them off?" Betty's disarming reply won the day for Flynn: "I didn't have no objections." Errol Flynn was acquitted on all four counts.

Gentleman Jim, released shortly after, turned out to be one of Flynn's finest vehicles, pleasing critics and public alike. This movie-star scandal, which only ten years previously would have surely meant career death, cancelled contracts and public dishonor — even if the main character had been acquitted — did not work out that way this time. "Morality" had shifted. Identifying fans liked the idea of being "In like Flynn" and turned out in droves for the movie. "Morality" had evolved so much by these wartime years, that the Flynn case would never have been brought to court, had it not been for concealed pressure — not pressure from the public.

The papers could not go into the underside of the affair at the time, but it soon became apparent to everyone involved, to Flynn, Geisler and Warner Bros., that the persecution of Flynn was traceable to corrupt Los Angeles politicians who had decided that the studios, after a shaky period during the Depression, were now making a fortune with wartime escapist entertainment movies and were not, it seemed to them, coming across with juicy enough "kickbacks." These pay-offs had been habitually turned over to the "Bosses" who would make sure that the police got its cut of the take. They, in turn, protected the studios, by dropping charges in case stars got into any sort of trouble.

The Flynn mountain would have remained a molehill, except that shortly before it broke, some changes had been made in the chain of command at L.A. City Hall. When Jack Warner had failed to cough up to the new Bosses, the first rape charge against Flynn had been brought up as a warning; when that could not be substantiated, the second chippie was pushed forward by the cops to chirp her year-old charges.

Fortunately for Flynn, the jury (Geisler had made sure that nine of the twelve were women) did not buy the police's trumped-up case, and Errol Flynn was free — to delight his fans with more good flicks and to enjoy twenty more years of carousing.

Peggy, Flynn and Betty in court ↑   Errol: Ladies' Man at Sea →

·WHO'S DADDY?·
·SUGAR DADDY·

Jerry Geisler was soon to receive another call: a fifty-four-year-old millionaire in trouble with a girl. His name was Charles Spencer Chaplin. The opening scene of what was to become a long drawn out courtroom drama took place under the auspices of another millionaire: J. Paul Getty. It all began when Miss Plain Joan Barry arrived in Hollywood in 1940, expecting to crash the movies. Her name did make headlines in 1943 and 1944, not for any on-screen ability but because she was still expecting — and had named Charlie Chaplin as the father. She had floated around town taking odd jobs, often as a waitress. One day she was invited to join a party of girls who were going down to Mexico for the inauguration of oil-man Getty's Avila Camacho. There she met Tim Durant, an agent for United Artists, who introduced her to Chaplin, then looking for a female lead for Shadow and Substance, a film he was planning.

Chaplin told the press he had discovered a new Maude Adams and he signed Barry up for a seventy-five-dollar-a-week contract. While being groomed for the role, the budding star underwent two abortions. By the following year, in October 1942, Chaplin's dissatisfaction with her,

both personal and professional, seemed complete. Her salary was reduced to $25. The girl turned up at his house at Christmas, brandishing a gun she had bought at a pawnshop. The master actor and director found these histrionics an erotic turn-on; he dispensed with the pistol and balled his deranged, estranged protégée on a bearskin rug in front of a glowing fireplace. When she turned up again to make a scene a few days later, the Great Dictator called the police who ordered her to leave town. A few months later she was discovered climbing into a window at Chaplin's house and given thirty days in jail.

Then the storm broke — thanks to the power of one of Chaplin's most bitter enemies. Hedda Hopper and Louella Parsons, two battle-axe columnists, were as famous in their heyday as gorgeous Garbo or Marlene and the other stars whose lives they wrote about. They were, however, much more powerful, and had set themselves up as the arbiters of the film colony's moral life. Through their syndicated columns they reached 75,000,000 readers and exerted an influence difficult to imagine today in a more liberated society which no longer considers the revelation that a married star has been seen out with a

---

← Chaplin and Joan Barry in court: No love lost

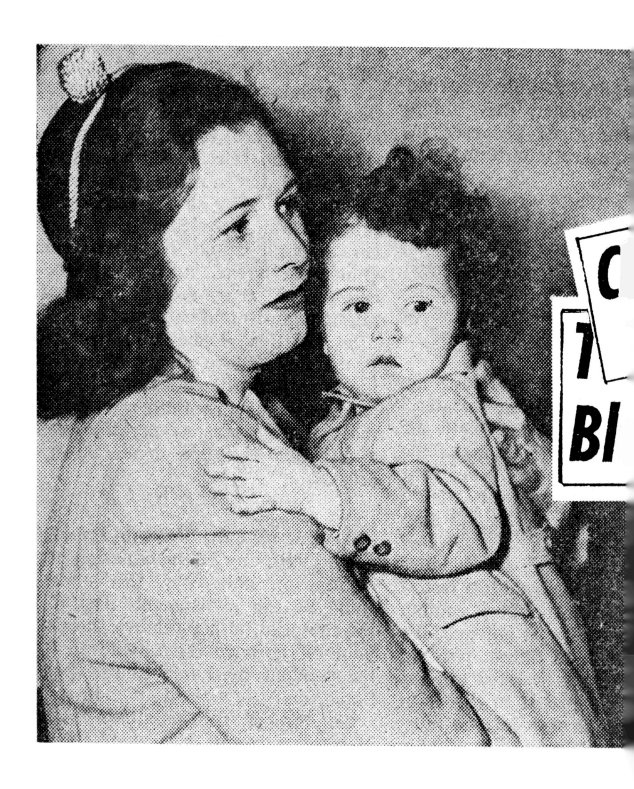

lin Jury Hears Doctors Say
od Tests Ruled Out Charlie

Chaplin Judge Rules--
d Tests Not Binding,

young chorus girl as news on a par with the explosion of the first atom bomb.

Hedda, in particular, had for many years treated Chaplin as an enemy of society. Her patriotic hackles up, she denounced him for having arrived a poor unknown in the United States, making a fortune here and then never becoming an American citizen. One morning, while Hedda was relieving herself of the day's tittle-tattle to her secretary, an hysterical redhead barged in and blurted out that she was bearing Charlie Chaplin's illegitimate child and had been thrown out by him. This was the biggest grist that had ever hit Hedda's mill. Joan said she had come to her because she had read one of her columns in which Hedda had warned of the fate awaiting any girl foolish enough to accept a position as a Chaplin protégée.

Hedda's next column spewed forth the news, as a warning to other film folk involved in "dubious relationships." Plain Joan's pregnancy rapidly stirred up a bitchy media tug-of-war. Charlie postponed his marriage to Oona O'Neill because of Hedda's story. As revenge on Hedda, when he later married Oona, he gave the scoop to "Lolly" in order to rub salt into Hedda's acid tongue. Hardly a day went by without a blast from Hopper at Charlie. She let fly rumors that Chaplin had insulted the press at his wedding, calling them "morons" (untrue), that Shadow and Substance would be cancelled, that the forthcoming paternity trial would be the biggest Hollywood circus in years.

When the suit was filed, Chaplin denied that he had fathered the child but agreed to submit to a blood test. He paid all of Barry's medical expenses, gave her $2500 and a hundred a week as settlement. Chaplin was then indicted by a federal grand jury on four counts. The F.B.I. entered the case. Chaplin was photographed being fingerprinted.

Barry's daughter was born on October 2, 1943. The decision was a model of perplexity. Although blood tests proved that Chaplin was not the girl's father, the jury, despite all Geisler's efforts, decided against him and ordered him to support the child. It is interesting to note that while Louella published the results of the blood tests, Hedda was on the spot covering the trial, but made no mention of them.

More fodder was furnished Chaplin's right-wing enemies when, during the trial, a Chaplin festival was launched in Moscow. The Russians opened the festival by blaming Chaplin's recent troubles on the Trotskyites! They were to blame, and with them the "mud-slingers of the Hearst and McCormick tabloid press." This was a unique event — the only time in recorded history when the Kremlin had stuck its two kopecks into a Hollywood sex scandal.

Hedda continued needling Chaplin for the rest of her life. But towards the end of her career, her opinions, and those of her rival sister-in-twaddle, Lolly Parsons, were fortunately no longer received by a more sophisticated American public as engraved footnotes to The Ten Commandments.

Genius is often an infinite capacity for survival. Chaplin survived his trials and other tribulations, and went on to make four films, one of which, Monsieur Verdoux, although financially a disaster (it was banned in many places in the United States), incorporated a great deal of his bitterness. The result was a masterpiece, one of the finest films ever made. It will be seen and admired long after the Heddas and Louellas are forgotten.

Chaplin, Joan and daughter in court →

220

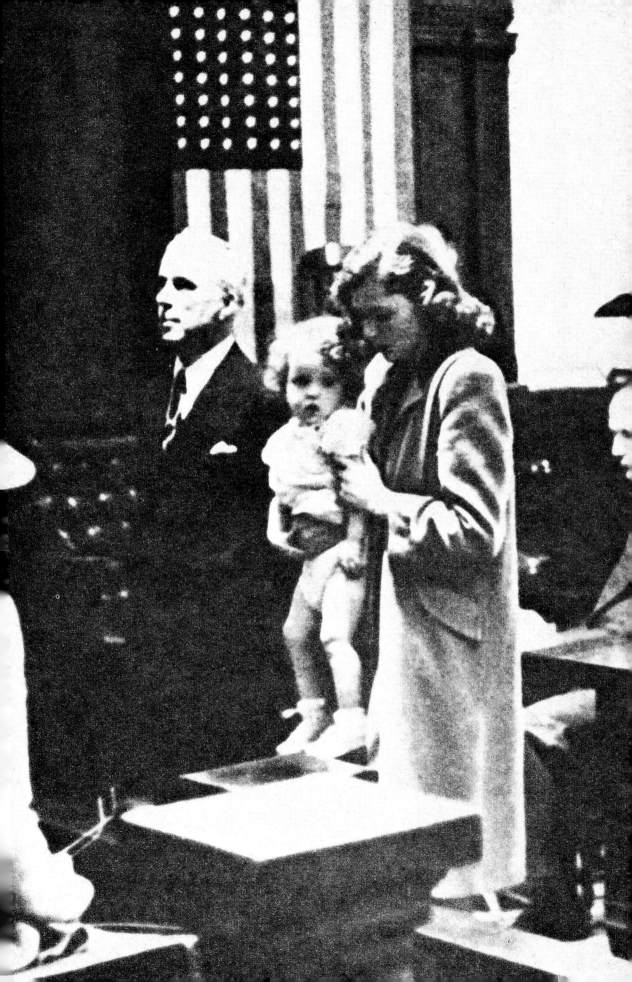

·DAUGHTER OF FURY·
·FRANCES, SAINT·

The spectacular crack-up of the beautiful, sensitive and highly strung actress, Frances Farmer, supplied another real-life Movieland drama which in 1943 competed with the Chaplin–Barry fracas and a little thing like World War II for headlines in papers throughout the country.

In 1935, after she had won a magazine popularity contest, Paramount snapped up the "New Garbo" for a seven-year contract. Frances, who considered herself a serious actress and dreamed of appearing in Chekhov and the classics (she later did work for a spell with the Group Theatre in New York, starring in Golden Boy and The Fifth Column, working with Elia Kazan and Clifford Odets) found herself cast by the studio opposite Bing Crosby in Rhythm on the Range, side by side with Martha Raye and Bob Burns and his bazooka. She was loaned out to Goldwyn (Paramount made a large profit on such loan-outs, not a penny of it going to Frances) for a costumer, Come and Get It. Then followed: Son of Fury, with Tyrone Power, Ebb Tide with Ray Milland, The Toast of New York with Cary Grant, and her most curious film, Among the Living, with Albert Dekker. The would-be Method actress was then thrust into South of Pago Pago with John Hall.

Frances won no more popularity contests while in Southern California. A resolute individualist who refused to "go Hollywood," she was often quoted as saying she hated everything about the place except the money. She made an enemy of Zukor and other moguls, and when her time of trouble came in 1943, many felt it was a case of a smart aleck getting her deserved comeuppance.

Her breakdown was triggered by a banal incident, an arrest for a minor traffic violation in Santa Monica the night of October 19, 1942. She was charged with drunk driving without a license, and with having her lights on in a dim-out zone on the Pacific Coast Highway. Frances was a cop-hater; from this moment on the fuzz became her personal externalized demons. She responded to the patrolman's arrogance and insults with equal hostility, and the shouting match ended with her being dragged off to the Santa Monica jail. In night court she was sentenced to one hundred and eighty days and put on probation. (If ever a damsel in distress needed the services of a Jerry Geisler, Farmer was she.)

Not too long after, she was arrested at Hollywood's Knickerbocker Hotel for having failed to report to her parole officer; this came on the heels of an hysterical fling,

---

← Frances Farmer: Individualist

during which she had dislocated the studio hairdresser's jaw, lost her sweater in a boozy night-club brawl and streaked topless through traffic down Sunset Strip. The police revved up her paranoia by loudly beating on her door, then entering with a passkey with gun and handcuffs at the ready. She hid in the bathroom. The cops broke down the bathroom door and, after a wild struggle, carted her off naked through the Knickerbocker lobby.

At Hollywood police headquarters, the officers got a jolt when the "New Garbo" signed "Cocksucker" as her occupation.

In court for sentencing, she

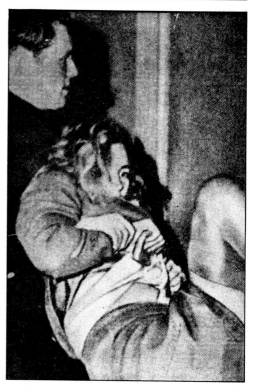

stared at the mob of photographers gathered around her and spat out, "Rats! Rats! Rats!" When the judge asked how she had lost her sweater in the night-club brawl, she denied any knowledge of the affair. When His Honor asked her about the extent of her drinking, she replied, her voice rising:

"Listen, I put liquor in my milk. I put liquor in my coffee and in my orange juice. What do you want me to do, starve to death? I drink everything I can get, including benzedrine."

Beet-faced Judge Hickson was no kindly Judge Hardy. He rose from his chair and belched out the one-hundred-and-eighty-day sentence.

"Fine!" Frances shouted back at him, adding, "Have you ever had a broken heart?" (She was referring to her unpleasant affair with Clifford Odets and her recent divorce from Leif Ericson.)

She then tossed an ink pot at His

PHILADELPHIA RECORD,

Frances Farmer on Rampage in Court —Floors Policemn and Goes to Jail

Actress Tells Judge She Put Liquor in Her Milk, Orange Juice and Coffee.

HOLLYWOOD, Jan. 14 (UP)—Screen Actress Frances Farmer, who told a police court Judge she puts liquor in her milk, in her coffee and in her orange juice, was sentenced today to 180 days in jail after a hectic court appearance during which she knocked down a policeman.

The 29-year-old actress was arrested last night for violation of a probation imposed upon her following a conviction of driving an automobile while intoxicated.

Hysterical Fling.

Her arrest ended a 24-hour hysterical fling, during which she was accused of dislocating a hairdresser's jaw and participating in a night club argument.

Brought before Police Judge Marshal Hickson today, Miss Farmer was a defiant mood. He asked her if she had reported to her probation officer.

"No," she replied. "He didn't come around and see me."

Admits Fighting.

The Judge asked if she was in a fight Tuesday night at the Knickerbocker Hotel.

"Yes," she said. "I was fighting for my country as well as myself."

"Have you driven a car since you were put on probation?" she was asked.

"No, I haven't," she snapped back. "But only because I couldn't get my hands on one."

Asks About Drinking.

She said she didn't know anything about charges that she was in a night club since Tuesday and lost her sweater in the fracas. The Judge attempted to query her again as to the extent of her drinking.

"Listen," she said, her voice rising, "I put liquor in my milk. I put liquor in my coffee and in my orange juice. What do you want me to do, starve to death? I drink everything I can get, including benzedrine."

Judge Hickson rose from his chair and shouted out the 180-day sentence.

Hints Broken Heart.

"Fine," Miss Farmer shouted back at him, adding: "Have you ever had a broken heart?"

Then she walked quietly to a room outside the courtroom and asked to use the telephone. When she was denied this request, she swung at a police matron. Two policemen hurried to aid the matron, and in the struggle one was knocked down.

The policemen took off Miss Farmer's shoes to soften her kicks. Finally, she was carried in a straitjacket to a cell. She continued to scream and kick.

Who Wrote Script.

When the actress was brought before Captain Charles Fitzgerald, of the county jail staff, she included him in her tirade.

"Why can't you be nice?" Fitzgerald asked her.

"Who wrote your script?" she snapped back, "and why in hell don't you get that potbelly off of you?"

"I got that from eating, not drinking," was Fitzgerald's reply.

Miss Farmer looked at the corps of press photographers gathered around her and said:

"Rats! Rats!"

She's an Actress.

When she was asked her occupation she answered:

"I'm an actress, you know that—Fools!

"Just put me down as a vag—a vagrant vagabond."

Then she asked to be taken to her cell.

"Show me where I'm going to live. I want to get in there and brush my teeth and begin to live my 180 days," she said.

Searched 2 Weeks.

Police said they had been searching for Miss Farmer for two weeks.

Detective Earl Reinbold woke her in a fashionable Hollywood hotel yesterday to take her into custody. He said she fled into a bathroom and made her reappearance in the nude. At police headquarters she listed her occupation as such an unorthodox one that it caused the police booking officer to jump when she read it.

Edna Burge, a studio hairdresser, charged that Miss Farmer hit her so hard she had to have her jaw set before she could close her mouth.

Removed From Role.

The Monogram Studio later disclosed that Miss Farmer had been removed from the lead role of "No Escape" and Mary Brian has been substituted.

The sweater incident was revealed by Emily Grinnell, an aircraft worker who said she was attempting to quiet Miss Farmer at a night club and that the actress slid from her chair "and left her sweater in my arms."

Divorced Last Fall.

Miss Farmer, a graduate of the University of Washington, first broke into the movies eight years ago when she won a popularity contest. She has been active during the last few years in left-wing activities in New York, Philadelphia and Hollywood.

She was divorced last fall in Reno by actor Leif Erickson.

May Be Publicity Stunt, Says Mother of Actress

SEATTLE, Jan. 14 (UP)—Mrs. E. M. Farmer said today the parole violation difficulties of her actress daughter, Frances, may be only a publicity stunt designed to give her the true-to-life experience of a jail inmate.

Play With Jail Scenes.

"They might be planning a picture for her with jail scenes in it and want to be able to give a performance based on actual experience," Mrs. Farmer said.

"If it isn't a publicity stunt, then this is Frances' first serious trouble. She was a model child."

Drinking Is Trouble.

Told that the actress testified she had been "drinking all the liquor I could get my hands on," Mrs. Farmer said:

"Of course, that's Frances' trouble. She does it as an escape from herself and her frustrations. She has had bad advice in her professional life from people more interested in her money-making abilities than in her personal welfare."

FRANCES FARMER
She was arrested for violating her probation in a drunken driving case.

—Associated Press Wirephoto.

Honor's head — with stunning accuracy. Her request to make a phone call on leaving the courtroom was unreasonably refused; this provoked Frances to swing at a police matron and floor a policeman. She was carried to her cell in a straight jacket.

No help was forthcoming from her current employer, Monogram Pictures. (By then, Frances had skidded from her Pinnacle at Paramount to the Nadir of Poverty Row.) Monogram hastened to replace Frances with Mary Brian as the lead in No Escape.

She desperately needed professional help. None was forthcoming. Instead, her mortal enemy, her Nemesis from the past, piped up: her mother. Mrs. Lillian V. Farmer (who had never wanted a child) told reporters in Seattle that her daughter's difficulties were only a publicity stunt designed to give her some real experience in the clink. "They might be planning a picture for her with jail scenes in it, this way she can give a performance based on actual experience," Mama lovingly blurted out.

Dear Mama Farmer (she seems to have crawled out of some very grim fairy tale) wiggled her fat ass down to Hollywood, declared her daughter a mental incompetent and signed the commitment papers. She blamed Frances' nervous breakdown on World Communism.

Frances had refused to accept work detail in prison. From there, she was now shoved into a private sanitarium to face the gruelling prospect of daily insulin shock treatments for three months (a treatment which has since been thoroughly discredited). After the

Frances: Defiance

horrors of the sanitarium, ten years of utter hell in the Snake Pit lay ahead. She was adjudged insane in 1944 and confined to the State Loony Bin at Steilacoom, Washington, her home state. (Be it ever so humble . . .)

Her confinement there was the most gruesome ordeal any screen personality was ever forced to endure — the most unbearably tragic of all Hollywood tragedies. She had been unhappy in the Purgatory of Hollywood, where her talent felt "constricted" by silly, superficial roles in dopey movies. Her merciless stars delivered her unto the Hell of straight jackets, leather straps and raping, sadistic bull-dike guardian devils. Come and Get It, indeed.

Her downfall brought forth little compassion in the Glamor Town which had exploited her. She had been a difficult "troublemaker"; they were glad to be rid of her. (William Wyler once went on record as saying, "The nicest thing I can say about Frances Farmer is that she is unbearable.") And to boot, she had been a pinko.

One single columnist spoke up in her behalf. That was John Rosenfield,

at the time of her initial arrest:

WHAT HAPPENED TO FRANCES FARMER SHOULDN'T HAVE HAPPENED AT ALL

Just when the movie industry is winning the public's admiration, Hollywood breaks out in a rash of petty scandals. It is not a tribute to a part of the press that some of these episodes have been played well beyond their merits as news.

It was the lesser part of sagacity that the industry permitted some of these affairs to get out of hand. The Frances Farmer Incident should never have happened. This unusually gifted actress was no threat against law and order or the public safety. Something that began as merely a traffic reprimand grew into a case of personal violence, a serious charge and a jail sentence.

And all because a sensitive high-strung girl was on the verge of a nervous breakdown.

Miss Farmer, who is no prodigy of emotional stability or sound business management, needed a lawyer one unhappy night last winter. A helping hand might have extradited her immediately from nothing more than a traffic violation. The terrible truth is that she stood alone, and lost.

Rosenfield's was the only note of compassion. The rest of the press coverage followed the lethal lead of Lolly Parsons, who snickered: "Hollywood Cinderella Girl has gone back to the ashes on a liquor-slicked highway."

Genius and Madness compose Janus-faced creativity. Of all the Hollywood Magdalenes who have drunk at the well of madness — Clara Bow, Gail Russell, Gene Tierney — we nominate as their patron, Frances, Saint.

Frances Farmer: Paramount Pretty ↑   Frances: Committed to Hell →

· CHOP-SUICIDE ·

The Suicide Syndrome surfaced again in the Forties with the sleeping-pill deaths of Julian Eltinge in 1941, and the death of sad clown Joe Jackson in 1942.

The Seconal suicide of Lupe Velez in 1944 received the lion's share of headlines. Lupe had been a part of the Hollywood scene since the late Twenties, when the go-getting teenager had come up from Mexico City to conquer the movies. She was spotted by Doug Fairbanks, who gave her the lead opposite him in The Gaucho, and she was on her way. Lupe soon earned the pet name "Mexican Spitfire" for her irrepressible gaiety and fiery temper.

She lost no time in assaying the Hollywood Male. Her first affair was with John Gilbert (who needed a strong rebound antidote to Garbo). In 1929 she took up with her Wolf Song leading man, young buck Gary Cooper. Theirs was a wild affair, but after several months of Lupe's insatiable, pungent tantrums, an exhausted Coop begged out. When a startling specimen of manhood named Johnny Weissmuller arrived in Hollywood still wet from his L.A. Olympics swimming triumph, Lupe zeroed in, and Tarzan found a mate in a tempestuous union that lasted till their divorce in 1938. Always

the child, Lupe just couldn't understand why Johnny would get mad when she'd flash her charms at Hollywood parties by flinging her dress over her head — she was always innocent of lingerie.

Their raucous spats at home could often reach the perked ears of snoopy Hedda, right across the street. Their most public tiff occurred one night at Ciro's when Johnny tossed a food-laden table at Lupe's meowing puss. The love-hate madness of their intense passion often left Lupe marks on Weissmuller's godlike torso, strawberry hickies on that Thor throat, annular bites on his perfect pecs, eloquent scratches on his ivory back. The make-up man on MGM's Tarzan sets had his work cut out for him. It was a rare Hollywood example of married Amour Fou.

After the inevitable divorce from Weissmuller, Man-Addict Lupe's tortured flings were frequent and brief. From stars her sights slipped to featured players to cowboys to stuntmen to the parasitic crowd of Hollywood he-men hangers on, professional older-dame pleasers, studs on the take whose gig was gigolo. Her career also skidded from A's to B's, to quickie Mexican Spitfire farces with Leon Errol, in which she

---

← Lupe: Tarzan's mate

served Chile-con-Lupe parodies
of her own spicy persona.

Tiny Lupe was not happy. Less Big
than she once was, her Loves
were now bought. Though she still
looked the elfin gamine, she
knew she was thirty-six.

Then her periods stopped and she
realized that Harald Ramond,
her latest, had knocked her up.

Big Deal? Call for Doctor Killkare
(the joke name for Tinsel Town's
leading abortionist)? Forget it. Lupe,
the gyrating cunt-flashing Hollywood
party girl, was in her Heart of
Hearts the snow-white virgin of her First
Communion in San Luis Potosi,
an awed adorer of Nuestra Señora dos
Grandes Dolores, an on-your-knees
girl! Like her buddy, Novarro.
Devout Mexican Catholic.

She could not bear to snuff the
gigolo's fetus within her. Rather,
she would doom herself to
Eternal Torments by committing
Her Own Murder, by Herself. (The
punishments awaiting her for
that could not be worse than the
still-of-the-night void, the
miss-Johnny emptiness suffered
every second in her prison–mansion on
North Rodeo Drive.)

The mortgage was overdue on
this outmoded Zorro-era pile. Lupe was
by now completely zonked by
debt. (Like Wagner, like Wilde, like
Isadora, she belonged to that
skittish-ecstatic coterie, the Creditors-
be-Damned School, the World-
Owes-Me-Everything Elite.)

Back in '44, a star name could still
attract grocery and deli credit
in the newly rich township of Beverly
Hills. So, the motorized charge-account
chariots wended their way to
Lupe's hacienda, laden with bubbly
and gourmet Mexican delights,
the spicy makings of a sumptuous
Días Dos Muertes feast. Enough
fresh flowers arrived to smother a

gangster's funeral: massed
gardenias, sheaves of tuberoses,
emitting fragrances to make an
army faint.

All on account. (Sign here, please
Miss Velez.) Of course, she'd
never pay: what are pequeño venial
sins in Inferno, against the
Heavy she was signing for?

Lupe planned her Last Night on
Earth as punctiliously as an
early De Mille Allegorical Flashback.
(The Spitfire had told her loaded
companions at the Troc three
nights before, as she downed her
tenth Tequila Sunrise: "I know
I'm not worth anything, I can't sing
well, I can't dance." She snagged
the waiter for another round: ". . . and
it comes from mi corazón . . . or
I wouldn't say these things."
Consummate actress off screen, she
cued her pals for the horrified
denials, the eyes-imploring-heaven
Greco glances, the desperately
desired fair flattery, heartfelt praise:
"No, no, dollink! You are vunnerfull,
Lupita chérie!"

The Spitfire could not succeed in
obliterating the memory of the

On the Tarzan set: Irreplaceable Johnny Weissmuller →

Harald; Lolly could now have this scoop: It's All Off.

Louella recalled: "Lupe told me that she and Harald had had one big battle and she told him to get out of her house. And when I asked her how the runt spelled his name, she told me, 'I don't know. I never did know. Who cares?'"

Lupe invited her two best gal pals, Estelle Taylor (Jack Dempsey's ex) and Benita Oakie (wife of Jack) to share a Last Supper. After the Mexican feast, over brandy and cigarillos, Lupe 'fessed up: "I'm tired of life. I have to fight for everything. I'm so tired of it all. Ever since I was a baby in Mexico, I've been fighting. It's my baby. I couldn't commit murder and still live with myself. I would rather kill myself."

The Spitfire found herself alone again at 3 AM in the big fake hacienda on North Rodeo Drive, and for the last time she ascended the wrought-iron staircase in her silver lamé gown (like the rest of it, unpaid for).

Cad, the Heartless Heel, her Nicky Arnstein, Harald Ramond — who'd knocked her up and taken the news with his get-lost look, his so-what shrug. Harald was darkly handsome, tall and hung. But he was no caballero — what did she expect from the Cinebar School of Chivalry?

Ramond had phoned Lupe's manager, Little Bo Roos, stating he would agree to a mock ceremony on the condition that Lupe signed a document stating she knew he was marrying her solely to provide a name for Her Baby.)

When Roos conveyed this bummer to Lupe, she stormed and called Lolly Parsons. It had been Lolly who had announced her engagement to

← Lupe, Chips and Clayton Moore — a "Johnny" substitute

Her bedroom was Our Lady of Guadalupe's Chapel on her Day of Days: flowers, candles, everywhere—everything aglow. Waiting for the Star. She pencilled a farewell note on a memo pad on the night table, by the white-gold telephone:

To Harald,
    May God forgive you and forgive me, too but I prefer to take my life away and our baby's before I bring him with shame or killin him.
                        LUPE

Then, on the back of the sheet, she pencilled an afterthought:

How could you, Harald, fake such a great love for me and our baby when all the time you didn't want us? I see no other way out for me so goodbye and good luck to you.   Love,
                        LUPE

She opened the bottle of Seconal that stood on the night table, picked up the water glass, then swallowed the seventy-five little Tickets to Oblivion. She stretched out on the satin bed beneath the great crucifix, hands joined on her breast in a last prayer, closed her eyes and envisioned the next day's front-page photos: Sleeping Beauty. And, of course, Louella's exclusive of the Farewell Scene, in a page-one, black-bordered box.
    And, indeed, in the next day's

Lupe's Mexican Spitfire: Self-parody ↑

237

<u>Examiner</u>, Lolly O. described the Still Life Discovered at Casa Felicias, North Rodeo Drive:

"Lupe was never lovelier as she lay there, as if slumbering . . . A faint smile, like secret dreams . . . Looking like a child taking nappy, like a good little girl . . . Hark! there are the doggies, there's Chops, there's Chips, scratching at the door . . . They're whimpering, they're whining . . . They want their little Lupita to take them out to play . . ."

No accompanying death-bed photo of Lupe appeared to match Parsons' prose. The actual scene had been something else.

When Juanita, the chambermaid, had opened the bedroom door at nine, the morning after the suicide, no Lupe was in sight. The bed was empty. The aroma of scented candles, the fragrance of tuberoses almost, but not <u>quite</u> masked a stench recalling that left by Skid-Row derelicts. Juanita traced the vomit trail from the bed, followed the spotty track over to the orchid-tiled bathroom. There she found her mistress, Señorita Velez, head jammed down in the toilet bowl, drowned.

The huge dose of Seconal had not been fatal in the expected fashion. It had mixed retch-erously with the Spitfire's Mexi-Spice Last Supper. The gut action, her stomach churning, had revived the dazed Lupe. Violently sick, an ultimate fastidiousness drove her to stagger towards the sanitary sanctum of the <u>salle de bain</u> where she slipped on the <u>tiles and plunged</u> head first into her Egyptian Chartreuse Onyx Hush-Flush Model Deluxe.

This Scoop Macabre was the one that Louella had been sitting on.

Harald Ramond — the Heel — pays his last respects to Lupe ↑   Lupe: Sign-off note →

· MR. BUGS COMES TO TOWN ·

Handsome mobster Benjamin "Bugsy" Siegel, of the flashing teeth and baby blue eyes, had, during his heyday, more of Hollywood by the balls than ever any despotic director or dictatorial studio head. Siegel grew up in New York's Hell's Kitchen, side by side with George Raft; this boyhood friendship developed into a lifelong association. Bugsy started off like many another gangland punk, raping girls while still a teenager, housebreaking on his own hook. His start in organized crime was as a heroin pusher for Lucky Luciano; he got into bootlegging with Meyer Lansky during prohibition. The cold-blooded pro killer was always just underneath his good-looker mask; his libido was large, and as a young stud sexy psycho during the early Thirties, he provided many a hot night for Broadway showgirls.

With Lansky, Siegel participated in an unsuccessful plot to murder racket-busting prosecutor Thomas Dewey, then in the U.S. Attorney's office, later New York's Governor. In 1936, the New York gangland grapevine discovered that a Chicago mob was planning to move to the Coast to take over the Hollywood rackets, as yet not fully exploited. Gotham's hoodery decided to beat Chicago's to the gun. Bugsy went west with a half-dozen crime cronies. He rented the mansion of movie and Met Opera star Lawrence Tibbett.

Through his pal, George Raft, Siegel was introduced to the crème of Hollywood society, and was soon hobnobbing with Richard Barthelmess, Jean Harlow, Clark Gable, Gary Cooper and Cary Grant. During the early part of his stay Siegel's most lasting relationship was with the Countess Dorothy Taylor de Frasso, the wealthy socialite and party-giver. On arrival in Movieland, a few years before Bugsy, the Countess (who always got lots of space chez Hedda and Louella) found it an agreeable pastime to be ministress of Gary Cooper's charms — taking up where Lupe Velez left off. After Coop ditched her and married a younger woman, the Countess settled down in Bugsy's pants for a spell. One of Siegel's close "business" friends was the shady Marino Bello, Jean Harlow's stepfather. Bugsy was often taken to the Platinum Blonde's home by Bello; although Harlow never "warmed up" to him and resisted his advances, Siegel was the only big gangland figure present at her funeral in 1937.

By that same year, Bugsy's shakedown business which fed on Hollywood extras and bit players,

was going strong. It had been decided that these hordes of aspiring souls would have to pay off — or go without work. Bugsy worked both ends of the fatted calf and also made the moguls pay off. If they didn't, three hundred extras might "disappear" just when required by a producer for a mob scene. This racket netted Siegel half a million a year. The profits were put into his share of the Hollywood dope and white-slave traffics.

In 1939, Siegel, along with several others, was indicted for the murder of Harry Greenberg, a mobster associated with Lepke, who under the threat of a long sentence, had decided to "sing" and name names, places and details of crimes. Although Bugsy was held without bail, his power was such that he was given extraordinary V.I.P. treatment. He was given eighteen "exits" in a month and a half, popping in and out of jail as if it were a hotel. One day he was let out, handcuffed to a cop, for a "dental visit." He turned up at Lindy's Wilshire

Boulevard Café, handcuffed to his guard, who promptly checked the cuffs in the cloakroom so that Bugsy could have his hands free for a long afternoon "dental visit" with his current flame, British actress Wendy Barrie.

Charges against Bugsy for the Greenburg murder were soon dropped. His defender in this affair was Jerry Geisler, Hollywood's ace attorney, famed mouthpiece for Errol Flynn and Chaplin. An even more decisive incentive for his release was the fact that Siegel generously "donated" $50,000 to the re-election campaign of L.A. District Attorney Dockweiler.

Siegel had a wife stashed away, who mostly stayed out of the picture. His next and last big fling was with the notorious Virginia "Sugar" Hill, "Queen of the Mafia." This voluptuous ex-flea circus carny girl from Alabama had risen to some sort of fame in New York as the girl friend and hostess of "affairs" thrown by Luciano and Frank Costello. In 1941, she set up operations in Hollywood. Virginia ingratiated herself to Sam Goldwyn and got herself an acting plum in a great movie — a supporting role in Goldwyn's Ball of Fire, starring Gary Cooper and Barbara Stanwyck. Her liaison with the mobster had been in progress for several months by the time the picture was finished. Siegel was her escort to Ball of Fire's gala première and party, where the hoodlum lovers socialized with Dana Andrews, director Howard Hawks, Cooper and Stanwyck.

Later that year, when Bugsy was brought up on bookmaking charges, George Raft took the witness stand. He testified: "I've known Mr. Siegel for twenty years. We have been friends for a long, long time . . ." Georgie had always

been charmed by his pal's hypnotizing blue eyes. Later, when Bugsy was gunned down, the only long-standing friend he had left was the ever-faithful coin-flipping Raft. Through Raft, on his release, Bugsy became friendly with Georgie's irascible pal Leo Durocher, manager of the Brooklyn Dodgers, and Durocher's pretty wife, Mormon movie star Laraine Day.

Siegel will not go down in history for any of his sordid criminal activities — most of them were not that unique. But for better or worse, he has left a lasting Bugsy Monument on the face of the American Continent — that colossus of kitsch, Las Vegas. During the war years, oodles of money were being made in California. The public's desire for escapist entertainment had brought the movie industry out of the Depression and salaries were zooming, along with the loot from aircraft, munitions and black market profiteering. But at the same time, it was a period when the authorities were enforcing a major crackdown on crime and gambling. In 1944, Bugsy Siegel passed through Las Vegas. The town was then sleepy and undeveloped. Its city fathers were planning to preserve it as a kind of Far Western living Ghost Town, pushing for an ordinance which would oblige all new buildings to look like "Oater" movie sets in order to attract tourists in search of the quaint.

Siegel's grandiose scheme was to build the biggest hotel-casino in the United States. It would make Monte Carlo look like "peanuts." He borrowed several million dollars from several shady sources and in 1945 bought up the land surrounding a tacky hotel owned by a bankrupt widow. He moved in — with an army of architects, decorators, entertainers, and bandits with one and two arms. The Flamingo was born. Luxury building material was difficult to obtain in wartime, but never mind; Bugsy got in touch with Lucky Luciano, then exiled to his Italian patria. Luciano was able to smuggle out several tons of Carrara marble to send to Siegel for the Flamingo. The idea was to out-Miami Miami — and Bugsy did. The Metropolis of Super-Schlock arose out of the sands. Siegel implanted a style which flourished like a wild flaming out-of-control cancer in the Mojave Desert; one which continued to grow after his death to become the Vegas we all know and (perhaps) love, a demented highway of nouveau-riche Manic American Playboy.

The Flamingo was ready by Christmas, 1946 and cost $6,000,000. It was slow in earning its cost back, but Siegel was already showing signs of wanting to expand. To Nevadans it was apparent that he intended to take over not just Vegas, but the entire state. A few thousand new enemies were added to the long list of which Bugsy could boast.

After a lover's quarrel in Vegas,

Wendy Barrie and Virginia Hill: Gangsters' Molls

Virginia packed up and left town in spring 1947. She returned to California and rented a Spanish-Moorish castle in Beverly Hills, at 810 Linden Drive. Bugsy trailed after her and a semi-reconciliation was effected. She had accepted an invitation to travel around Europe with a wealthy French boy half her age. She left Siegel the keys to her house. Near midnight, June 20 of that year, Siegel was sitting in Virginia's living room reading a newspaper. A fiery blast suddenly shattered the window separating the living room from "Sugar's" garden. Bugsy Siegel lay on the couch, his ex-pretty face veiled in a thick sheet of blood, three bullets through his skull.

His deadly baby blue eyes would no longer fascinate the thrill-o-philes of Hollywood.

The police investigation got nowhere. Dozens of his ex-"colleagues" had reasons to want Bugsy out of the way. Although no indictments were forthcoming, it has since been established that he was murdered for not repaying the vast sums he had borrowed to construct the Flamingo.

Although he had often turned up at movie stars' funerals, not even a bit player turned up at his. He was buried in Beth Olam Cemetary close to the RKO studios — which like Bugsy Siegel would soon go out of business.

"Lucky" Luciano and target: Bye, bye, Blue Eyes

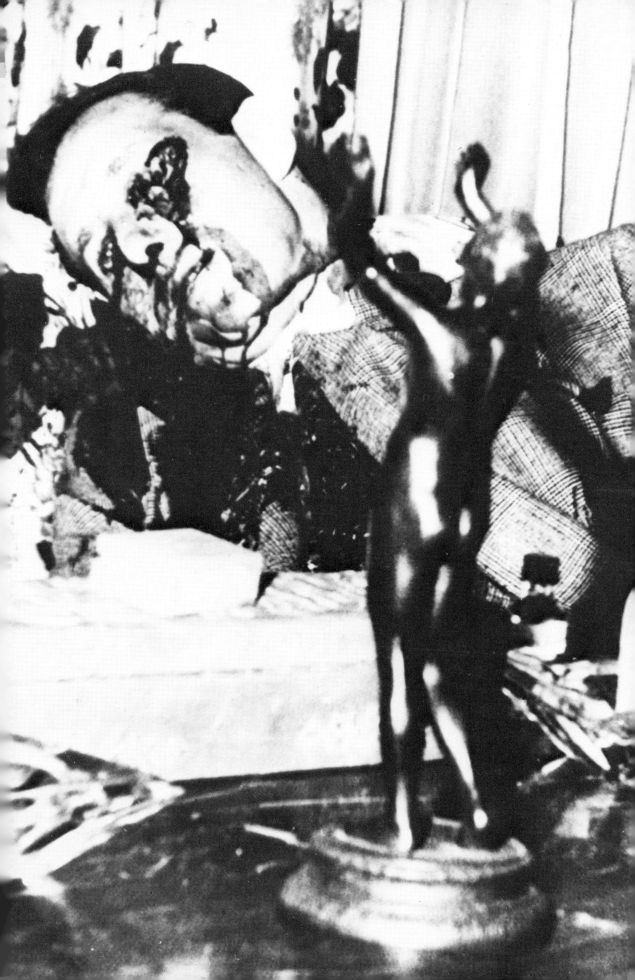

· RED TIDE ·

By 1947, the anti-Communist campaign led by Congressman J. Parnell Thomas had cast a pall over Hollywood as insidious as the newly pervasive Los Angeles smog. With the House Un-American Activities Committee granting them open season, Movieland's fanatical right wingers emerged from the woodwork, wrapped themselves in the flag and came out punching — generally below the belt. Mrs. Lela Rogers, dutiful daughter Ginger, and Howard Hughes were in the vanguard of the superpatriotic posse.

John Wayne was elected president of a lynching party which called itself the Motion Picture Alliance for the Preservation of American Ideals. Charles Coburn was first vice-president, Hedda Hopper second. (In 1947 Hedda spent her entire vacation travelling across the United States by car addressing women's clubs, urging them to boycott films which featured "Communist" actors.) Director Leo McCarey and actor Ward Bond were charter members of the Alliance. Paul Lukas, Robert Taylor, George Murphy and Adolphe Menjou were among those most eager to denounce all the Reds alleged to be hiding under Beverly Hills beds. (Menjou feared that a Communist take-over of the country was imminent. He declared that he was

moving to Texas . . . "because the Texans will shoot all Communists on sight.") That keen political analyst, Gary Cooper, boasted of having rejected "many scripts which espoused Communist ideas."

Aghast at these proceedings, a contingent of celebrities of another ilk chartered a plane and flew to Washington to protest these "invasions of citizens' rights to privacy in their beliefs." On the plane were: Bogart and Bacall, Gene Kelly, June Havoc, John Huston and Danny Kaye.

This stellar plane load did not play to an appreciative House. A group of arch fiends was shortly singled out — the Hollywood Ten. These were: Herbert Biberman, Albert Maltz, Edward Dmytryk, Adrian Scott, Ring Lardner, Jr., Samuel Ornitz, John Howard Lawson, Lester Cole, Alvah Bessie and Dalton Trumbo. (Irony of ironies: after his condemnation, Trumbo bumped into a fellow prisoner — none other than his former accuser, Congressman J. Parnell Thomas, who had been sentenced to time in the clink for payroll padding.) Allies of the ten who preferred self-imposed exile to the ignominy of the situation at home were the talented directors Jules Dassin, John Berry and Joe Losey, who continued their careers in Europe.

The fate of those who stayed at home was often darker. The black-

---

← Bogie and Bacall: Two against the tide

list ruined the lives or cut short the careers of such fine talents as Anne Revere, Gale Sondergaard, Jean Muir, John Garfield and J. Edward Bromberg. Dashiell Hammett and Lillian Hellman faced the inquisitors with dignity and honor; bullfrog-voiced actor Lionel Stander did a bang-up number of outraged innocence for the committee's benefit, and told them where to go. He then cleared out to Italy, where he continued his eccentric career unperturbed. Sidney Buchman, scenarist of Capra's Mr. Smith Goes to Washington, refused to appear. He was cited for contempt of Congress and immediately became unemployable in Hollywood.

Conscience is a sometimes thing and did not make cowards of them all. But some celebrities squealed, named names and blithely continued their careers through this Dark Age: Dmytryk, Elia Kazan, Jerome Robbins. Larry Parks was a special case. He admitted to membership in the Communist Party to save his skin. His skin may have been saved, but his career was finished.

The public was not amused. For it, politics and Hollywood just didn't mix. The Red Hunt did nothing to improve the quality of American films or American life. What it did do was ruin many lives and careers and tarnish the glamor of Tinsel Town.

John Garfield: Blackballed ↑   Gale Sondergaard: Career cut short →

·PEEP SHOW PECCADILLOS·

Mr. and Mrs. Moviegoer were more interested in the hullabaloo caused by the Fourth-of-July suicide of Carole Landis in 1948, provoked by unrequited love for Rex Harrison. Rex found Carole's body lying on the bathroom floor of her Pacific Palisades home, her head resting on a jewel box, one hand clutching a crumpled envelope that still contained a sleeping pill. On the vanity table of her bedroom a note was found addressed to her mother:

Dearest Mommie:
I'm sorry, really sorry, to put you through this. But there is no way to avoid it. I love you darling. You have been the most wonderful mom ever. And that applies to all our family. I love each and every one of them dearly. Everything goes to you. Look in the files and there is a will which decrees everything.
Goodbye, my angel.
Pray for me.

Your baby.

A short time before, Carole Landis had confessed to Photoplay: "Let me tell you this: Every girl in the world wants to find the right man, someone who is sympathetic and understanding and helpful and strong, someone she can love madly. Actresses are no exceptions; glamour girls are certainly no exceptions. The glamour and the tinsel, the fame and the money mean very little if there is a hurt in the heart."

Another hullabaloo surrounded the arrest of Robert Mitchum the night of August 31, 1948 for possession of marijuana, after a raid on the Hollywood cottage of Lila Leeds, a blonde starlet friend. The bust caused the cancellation of Bob's appearance the following day on the steps of Los Angeles City Hall, where he was scheduled to address a gathering for National Youth Week. Laconic Mitchum served a two-month jail sentence. When he emerged his popularity was absolutely unaffected, and Howard Hughes of RKO bought his contract from Selznick for over $200,000.

That same season, Gertrude Michael, who in the Thirties had portrayed the glamorous Sophie Lang in a series of neat B's about a svelte lady jewel thief (in the bizarre 1934 musical, Murder at the Vanities, she stole the show singing "Sweet Marijuana"), was arrested one night for drunkenness on the beach at Venice. When discovered by the fuzz, alone and clutching a bottle of Scotch,

Gertie sobbed and muttered: "Leave me alone. I have no friends. I am all alone and everyone has forgotten me. I want to jump in the ocean." She was taken to the police station, where she pleaded further to the waiting photographers: "I'm not a poor man's Carole Landis, and will you please retouch my photographs so I won't look like Frances Farmer?"

The period was also enlivened by a public fracas in which producer Walter Wanger shot Jennings Lang in the groin. Lang was the paramour of Wanger's wife, Joan Bennett. The noted producer served out a term in the pokey as prison librarian. (This affair paralleled an earlier celebrity shoot-up in 1938, when blues singer Ruth Etting's insanely jealous ex, Moe "The Gimp" Snyder, shot Myrl Alderman, her accompanist-lover on her Hollywood doorstep.)

On February 2, 1950, Ingrid Bergman (still Mrs. Lindstrom) bore Signor Rossellini a beautiful son, Robertino. Her spirit of independence scandalized the American public; she chose to ride out the storm in Europe.

Gertrude Michael: Gone are the Days ↑   Mitchum emerges from lockup: Popularity unaffected →

· CON GAME ·

In 1951 the police raided a deluxe pleasure house nestled in the hills above Sunset Strip, apprehending its madam, Billy Bennett, and seizing her customers ledger. The ledger was to become famous, for it was a golden book of Hollywood celebrities, habitual clientele of the establishment, some of whom had left their Oscars on the mantelpiece in gratitude for "services rendered." (The tip-off came from some well-known restaurateurs along the Strip, who were outraged at Billy's plans to "go legit" and open a proper, swank, and competing restaurant on their high-toned turf.) Dozens of male stars, as well as producers and scenarists, suddenly took off for the four posters of the world, accepted work in Europe, or suddenly needed vacations. The studios applied pressure and succeeded in hushing the matter up; within a few months the "vacationers" trickled back to California.

In 1952, the movie capital had not entirely recovered from the Billy Bennett Affair when a little magazine, published in New York, appeared on newsstands all over the country. This new offspring of yellow journalism soon became the talk of the town and Confidential acquired a reputation as the worst kind of rag — but everyone read it anyway.

Its motto was, "Tells the Facts and Names the Names." Scandal sheets were nothing new. There had been successful professional gossipmongers for decades including the vicious Westbrook Pegler, malicious Walter Winchell, that holy terror Elsa Maxwell and of course Tinsel Town's own innuendo specialists, Hedda and Louella. But perfidious Confidential carried things further than any of the rumormongers had done, went into greater detail and did not hesitate to affirm that the stories it published were a faithful account of the facts.

Confidential's publisher, Robert Harrison, had conceived the idea for the magazine after watching the daily televised Kefauver crime investigations. When he observed that these journalistic reports on vice, crime and prostitution eclipsed all other programs in the ratings, he deduced that the public was hungry for gossip and that a publication which presented such material in a spicy manner and did, in effect, name names, would go over big.

Harrison had started out in the Twenties as an office boy of the Daily GraphiC, a scandal sheet which in many ways was a precursor of Confidential. He then worked for Martin Quigley, pious publisher of Motion Picture Herald, and on his own had put out a fetish series: Hi-Heeled-Women-with-Whips-type magazines,

It could only happen in Hollywood!

...when **LANA TURNER** shared a lover with **AVA GARDNER!**

The handsome bartender knew how to make Pink Ladies, but what's a guy to do when he walks in and finds two ladies in

By B. J. DUCHARM

SUPPOSE YOU COULD FI Gardner for a blind date to question! In the first place, who that gorgeous Gardner gal would ever to find her a man?

Hold on, though. You just don't kn Across the nation, from coast to coa unusual for a guy to dig up an ext buddy. Leave it to movieland to go t There it's all reversed — the glamour girl friends with a handsome hunk of I signing.

whose circulations were falling off by the time he conceived the Confidential idea. The first issue did phenomenally well, and sold 250,000 copies. At its peak, Confidential was selling four million copies on newsstands — a record for American "journalism."

Harrison embarked on a large-scale attack on the private lives of America's most famous citizens. His formula was simple: a well-known name, an unflattering photograph and a story, fairly short, which presented a sordid episode in a mocking humorous manner. He knew what his customers wanted. He confided to friends: "Americans like to read about things which they are afraid to do themselves."

With the success of the magazine, its victims were increasingly those Hollywood luminaries whose private lives were of most morbid interest to the public. Harrison set up an "agency" in Hollywood, run by his niece, Marjorie Mead. It was given

the pretentious moniker "Hollywood Research Incorporated." Shady shamuses, would-be starlets, has-been hams and faded journalists were hired to rattle, prattle and tattle. The success of Confidential enabled Harrison to pay up to $1000 per gossip item, assuring him a fine stable of spies. Sometimes eminent show-biz personalities themselves would be informants on colleagues. Mike Todd called Harrison from California to fill him in on a juicy story concerning Harry Cohn, much-hated president of Columbia.

Many "researchers" were call girls. In fact, the nucleus of the organization was the bevy of pin-up girls who adorned the bars of Sunset Strip. In bed, these high-priced floozies received the confidences of famous stars, while a miniature tape recorder inside their purse, left carelessly open on the bedside table, recorded by night the indiscretions devoured later by avid readers.

Hollywood Research unearthed

Celebrities under fire ↑   Jayne Mansfield: Revelations →

compromising photographs and films and made use of the latest technical refinements: infra-red and ultra-rapid film, high powered telephoto lenses. This was the fashion in which the domestic feuds of Anita Ekberg and Anthony Steele were snooped upon. When particularly compromising material had been gathered, an agent of Hollywood Research visited the star involved with a copy in hand. It was suggested to the victim that the original might be purchased. Some paid, panic stricken; others refused. Stories which were not bought out of existence included: "Lizabeth Scott Among the Girls," "Dan Dailey in Drag," "Errol Flynn and his Two-Way Mirrors," "The Best Pumper in Hollywood? M-M-M Marilyn M-M-Monroe!," "Joan Crawford and the Handsome Bartender."

This reign of terror lasted for four years. Considerable, but unacknowledged assistance was given Harrison by two of New York's established gossipists, Walter

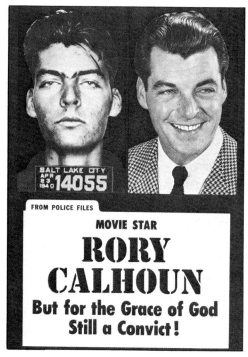

FROM POLICE FILES

MOVIE STAR
RORY CALHOUN
But for the Grace of God Still a Convict!

Winchell and Lee Mortimer. Mortimer, columnist and film critic for the now defunct Daily Mirror, would meet Harrison in a phone booth, slip him a juicy story, and if by chance they turned up that evening in the same nitery, the two men would pretend to be feuding and not speak to each other. Harrison often gave Winchell friendly plugs in the magazine, in stories in which someone else was given the axe (e.g. "Winchell was Right about Josephine Baker," etc.). In return, Winchell often plugged the magazine on television.

While the success and obscenities of Confidential increased with every issue, there was practically no film star who escaped its "revelations." Some were victims of a whole series of stories: Marilyn, Orson, Lana, Ava, Frank and Jayne. Ensconced in New York, Harrison made sure that each article was based on a piece of film or a tape recording, "evidence" which was checked by his shyster lawyers before publication. But with increasing success and no prosecutions, he began to embroider truth with picturesque details and overreached himself. He became one of the most hated men in the country. During a hunting expedition in Santo Domingo, someone took a few pot shots at him; one day Grace Kelly's father dropped into his New York office to smash up the place and take a poke at Harrison the day after an exposé had appeared about the future Princess of Monaco.

It was not until February of 1957 that a star finally had the courage to decide that enough was enough: Dorothy Dandridge filed suit against the magazine after an article appeared dealing with her alleged exploits in a forest in "naturalist" company. Dandridge asked

Confidential: Compromising material ↑

264

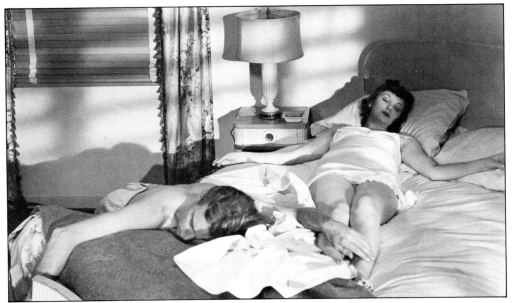

for two million dollars in damages.

With the firing of the first shot, the war was on: dozens of stars who had been slandered filed suits. When this happened, the movie-industry bigwigs decided that there was a new danger — the most important personalities of Hollywood would be quizzed in public about their private lives. The Grey Eminences once more attempted what had been successfully done in earlier scandals: hush it up.

Hollywood public relations man Robert Murphy was sent to the state capitol for talks with the Attorney General. He went so far as to threaten to withdraw the financial aid the movie industry was planning to grant to the next Republican campaign. But the state persisted in its plan to take action. Thus, many stars found it advisable to take a vacation. Clark Gable went to sunbathe in Tahiti, others took off for Europe or South America.

The trial finally started in Los Angeles, August 2, 1957. The press called it the "Trial of a Hundred Stars." Actually, after a brief appearance by Dorothy Dandridge,

who withdrew her complaint after a considerable out-of-court settlement, the trial counted only one other star — beautiful redhead Maureen O'Hara.

Confidential had informed its literati that Miss O'Hara had indulged in a "Chinese Chest" game in the plush seats of the loge section of Grauman's Chinese Theatre; her playmate was said to have been an attractive South American. Confidential related: "The usher saw a couple who heated up the balcony as if it were July. Maureen, blouse unbuttoned and her hair in disarray, had assumed, in order to watch the movie, the oddest posture ever to be beheld in the entire history of motion pictures. She was stretched out on three seats, the lucky South American occupying the middle chair, while a picture denouncing juvenile delinquency was being shown on the screen . . ." etc. etc. ad nauseam.

Judge Walker felt additional information was required. The scene was re-enacted in the balcony. The manager of Grauman's agreed to play the part of the South American, a young woman reporter was stand-in

Confidential: Spies in the bedroom ↑

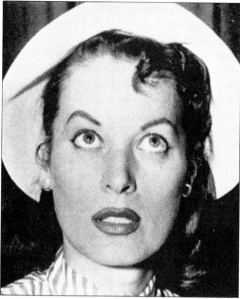

for the star. The manager sat down, the double stretched out, and even raised her legs in the air. The jury wanted further information. All twelve (including six dowagers) repaired to Row 35 where a minute examination of the three seats in question showed them no different from any others in the theater.

Maureen did not appear until August 17. She proved that at the time of the alleged frolics in the balcony of Grauman's she had been in Spain; her passport was entered as proof. She asked $5,000,000 in damages. The witnesses persisted, in spite of her passport proof of absence, insisting that it had been the actress they had seen in the loge. Her sister, an Irish nun, emerged from a convent to come to her defense. The Court brought in a lie detector, which did not prove that Maureen was telling the truth.

The hung jury finally reached a compromise. The obscenity charges were dismissed; Confidential only had to cough up $5000. There were many out-of-court settlements, however, which when added up, came to a lively sum. The magazine

paid $40,000 to Liberace — and almost as much to a dozen other celebrities.

The biggest actual drama of the case came with the suicide of Polly Gould, of the magazine's editorial staff. She killed herself the night of August 16; she was to testify the following day. It was then discovered that Polly had been playing a double game, selling the secrets of the magazine to the D.A. and informing Harrison of the maneuvers of the police.

Following the trial, Howard Rushmore, Harrison's editor-in-chief on Confidential (a paranoiac ex-Communist, Rushmore had recently started on an anti-Communist crusade), pulled out a gun while riding in a cab with his wife in New York's upper East Side, shot Mrs. Rushmore, then killed himself.

Harrison sold Confidential in 1957. Subsequently he started all over again, with a minor tabloid called Inside News. It didn't achieve its predecessor's fame. The days of this type of exposé were numbered. America's movie industry has declined; the public gets more mindless gossip than it can absorb daily on TV and, moreover, its shockability quotient has diminished. There are no longer more stars at MGM than in the Heavens. If that studio can be said to exist at all any more, it is as an empty planetarium. The few remaining movie celebrities are more than thankful to attract some attention by discussing their foibles themselves on TV talk shows. In fact, after the Confidential affair, stars like Errol Flynn, Zsa Zsa Gabor and Diana Barrymore started coming out with their own "tell-all" autobiographies. Why let others cash in on their private lives, when they could rake in the bread for it themselves? No magazine could continue to compete with that.

Maureen O'Hara: No Way ↑

The jury visits Grauman's →

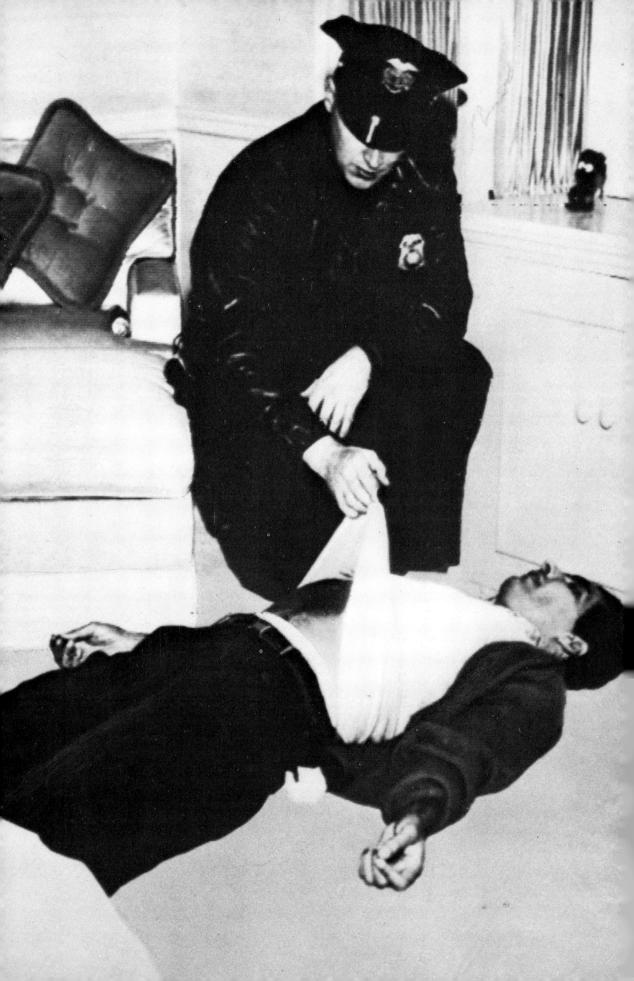

·BLOOD AND SOAP·

Jerry Geisler's phone rang on Good Friday, April 4, 1958; Hollywood's most famous lawyer heard a familiar voice: "This is Lana Turner. Something terrible has happened. Could you please come to my house?"

When Geisler arrived at the ex-Sweater Girl's colonial-style Beverly Hills mansion, Lana was in tears; her daughter Cheryl Crane was near hysteria. Geisler then saw the cause — the object harshly jarring with the pretty pinkness of Lana's boudoir: the bloodied corpse of Johnny Stompanato, alias Johnny Valentine, former bodyguard of gangster Mickey Cohen, notorious gigolo, Lana's latest lover.

Shortly after his arrival in Hollywood, handsome cocksure Stompanato had been sought by certain prominent ladies in the film colony; his own prominent endowment had earned him the sobriquet "Oscar" — after the foot-high Academy Award. In the spring of 1957, enterprising Johnny, who had never met Lana, obtained her private number and called her up. He knew, as did All America, that she had recently been separated from ex-Tarzan Lex Barker, and suspected she might be lonely and available. He suggested a blind date, mentioning the names of some mutual acquaintances and dropping a few hints about "Oscar."

At that time, he was operating a gift shop in Los Angeles. During the next fifteen months, he paid little attention to that business. Lana did not discover until after his death that Johnny had been married three times and had a ten-year-old son. She did know that he had solid connections with criminal elements, but Lana could not have cared less. Indeed, to have a real gangster for an escort, with a rod under his dinner jacket, added an extra thrill to the evening.

Lana was particularly vulnerable emotionally at this point in her life. After a dazzling career which had gotten off to a bang with a bit part in Warner's They Won't Forget in 1937 ("What a pair of tits!" was heard across the nation as schoolgirl Lana walked across the town square to be raped and murdered in the first reel of this epic. The rest of the film was an anticlimax.), she went from strength to strength. In 1946, Lana Turner was one of the ten biggest women money-makers in the country, and by the early Fifties was Queen of MGM. She also went from hombre to hombre. Her romances — Sinatra, Howard Hughes, Tyrone Power, Fernando Lamas — had filled the columns for two decades. Her

← Johnny in the boudoir: Jarring note

marriages had not really fulfilled her — Power was the only man she had really loved, and her possessiveness had ruined that affair. After bandleader Artie Shaw came Steve Crane (Lana was carrying Cheryl at the altar), then millionaire playboy Bob Topping. She had desperately wanted another child with her most recent husband, Lex Barker, but Lana miscarried. Following a run of bad films, after eighteen years at the studio, MGM had dropped her.

Her marriages and affairs had been dotted with violence, sometimes provoked or secretly desired. Lana had been thrown downstairs by one husband, slapped in public by another, drenched with champagne at Ciro's by a third. Once when she went out, her pretty face hidden behind dark glasses, it was to hide a black eye. She was quoted as saying, "I find men terribly exciting, and any girl who says she doesn't is an anemic old maid, a streetwalker or a saint." After thirty, this need for excitement became an obsession with Lana. During her separation from Johnny (she was making Another Time,

Another Place in England), the letters addressed to him showed the yearning for those "happy aches" he had knowingly inflicted. So she sent him a plane ticket — one of many gifts — and set him up in a big house in London on the "Street of Millionaires."

Johnny, certain of his power, became more and more demanding: "When I say HOP, you'll hop! When I say JUMP, you'll jump!" He also threatened to put his stamp on her. "I'll mutilate you, I'll hurt you so you'll be so repulsive you'll have to hide forever." At one point, Johnny came to the set and waved a pistol at Lana's co-star, Sean Connery, warning him to "stay away from Lana." Connery decked him. The studio, with a little help from Scotland Yard, had Stompanato ordered out of England.

Yet Lana missed Johnny. Her letters begged for his caresses: "So

---

Lana, Johnny, Cheryl ↑   Lana in They Won't Forget ↑   Lana and Johnny: Holiday in Mexico →

fierce that they hurt me . . . it is beautiful and yet it is terrible . . . I am yours and I need you, MY MAN!" The picture finished, their SM-esque affair was resumed in Mexico, where guests in nearby rooms at the Hotel Vía Vera complained of their noisy lovemaking. Then the return to Hollywood,

where Cheryl awaited them at the airport. Like many of the dream factory's offspring, the fourteen-year-old daughter of Lana and Steve Crane was a confused, disturbed teenager.

And one night in the big house on Bedford Drive, while Johnny abused Lana (she had refused to continue paying his gambling debts), threatening her with physical harm and swearing to revenge himself on her entire family, Cheryl listened at the door . . . "I'll cut you up and I'll get your mother and your daughter too . . . that's my business!"

Cheryl ran into the kitchen (according to her own and Lana's accounts), grabbed the first weapon she found — a nine-inch butcher knife — and rushed back to her mother's aid.

Lana later testified: "Everything happened so quickly that I did not even see the knife in my daughter's hand. I thought she had hit him in the stomach with her fist. Mr. Stompanato stumbled forward, turned

← Screen drama: Lana in love with gangster Robert Taylor in Johnny Eager

274

around and fell on his back. He choked, his hands on his throat. I ran to him and lifted up his sweater. I saw the blood . . . He made a horrible noise in his throat . . ."

Lana wept during this recital, almost fainted. She went on: "I tried to breathe air into his semi-open lips . . . my mouth against his . . ." Lana was near swooning. Geisler supported her. A bailiff brought her a glass of water. She finished, in a strangled voice: "He was dying."

The press was unanimous: the most dramatic scene of Lana's career. The jury was only out twenty minutes. Their verdict: justifiable homicide. The press had a field day; Lana's romantic past was raked up for inspection. Her love letters, discovered at Johnny's home by his hoodlum friends, were to furnish front pages across the land. Lana

was pilloried as a dissolute, unnatural mother by columnists, the clergy, sociologists and psychoanalysts. Cheryl was defended here, condemned there. "My heart bleeds for Cheryl!" wrote Hedda Hopper.

Walter Winchell was the only major columnist to take Lana's defense: "She is made of rays of the sun, woven of blue eyes, honey-colored hair and flowing curves. She is Lana Turner, goddess of the screen. But soon, the magician leaves and the shadows take over. All the hidden cruelties appear. She is lashed by vicious reporting, flogged by editorials, and threatened with being deprived of her child. And of course, it is outraged virtue which screams the the loudest. It seems sadistic to me to subject Lana to any more torment. No punishment that could be imagined could hurt her more than the

Lana on the witness stand ↑

memory of this nightmarish event. And
she is condemned to live with
this memory to the end of her days . . .
In short, give your heart to the
girl with the broken heart."

Old Glory Gloria Swanson was
infuriated by Winchell's defense of
Lana. She exploded: "Walter, I
think it is disgusting that you are trying
to whitewash Lana. You are not a
loyal American . . . you are washed up,
and everybody knows it except
you. As far as that poor Lana Turner is
concerned, the only true thing
you said is that she sleeps in a woolen
nightgown . . . she is not even an
actress . . . she is only a trollop."

The publication of Lana's letters
created a sensation. They had been
given by Mickey Cohen to an editor of
the Los Angeles Herald-Examiner
as revenge on Lana. Cohen, Johnny's
ex-boss and boy friend, had been
stuck for his funeral expenses. The

twelve letters (somewhat censored)
occupied the nation's front
pages for two days. As printed, they
seem less the work of a scarlet
woman than the outpourings of an
emotionally immature older
woman desperately in need of love.
Even with their plethora of asterisks,
it was the first time since the
publication of Mary Astor's diary that
the "inside" dirt of a movie star's
love life had been shovelled at
such length.

Lana rode out the storm. In many
theaters, when she first appeared
on screen in Peyton Place, the audience
applauded and shouted: "We're
on your side, Lana!" She went on to
make a slick soap opera for
producer Ross Hunter at Universal:
Imitation of Life, directed by
Douglas Sirk for Hunter, proved the
biggest box office success of
Lana's career.

Johnny's souvenirs: Guns and inscribed photos ↑   Lana's love letters made headlines →

New York Mirror

WEDNESDAY, APRIL 9, 1958

C

Bare Lana's Love Letters

STORY ON PAGE 3

'Love You —Lanita'

Burning letters from Lana Turner to Johnny Stompanato, knife-slain by her teen daughter, came to light yesterday. This is one of them. "We certainly are in tune—all the way," Lana says at one point. Below is a new photo of the actress. *(Another letter on Page 3)*

mon - afternoon

My Beloved love -
Just this morning your precious exciting letter arrived. and I'm quick jotting this to you to tell you I adore the way you write and all the truly beautiful things you say to me - So, please, please dearest continue. Every line warms me and makes me ache and miss you more each tiny moment - Its true - Its beautiful yet terrible But, just so, is deep love. Oh darling darling, the letter I wrote you last nite was so much in the same vein as yours I've just received - So you see we certainly are in tune - "All the Way" — I'll close now love, will write tonite - have to go to a meeting now with the dir. writers etc ——— Know how dearly I love you Angel Cudada y baci, baci, baci - Hold me dear lover mi macho - ciau, ciau papa - love you
Lanita

· HOLLYWOODÄMMERUNG ·

By the Sixties, Old Hollywood had died. The battlements of those feudal fiefdoms, the studios, fell one by one to the enemy. RKO was taken over by television, with Howard Hughes, once the property was unloaded, pronouncing this obit: "Hollywood is through." Fans rushed to the Fox auction (Gable's bathing suits, Ty Power's sword, who has you now?) and the MGM auction (Judy's high-button shoes from St. Louis, Garbo's Two Faced Woman ski suit, what freak fan or fanatic is wearing you at this moment, parading up and down in front of what broken mirror of the mind?). Fox's New York Street now only exists in memory. They have huffed and puffed and blown Andy Hardy's house down. And yet. . . .

Marilyn's suicide by sleeping pills in 1962 echoed the willed oblivions of so many others — Lupe, Carole Landis, Abigail Adams, Lynne Baggett, Laird Cregar . . . and many more. Marilyn had been out of control. (Had she ever really in her life been in control?) The fiefdoms had been losing hundreds of thousands of pieces of green from the tardiness, the non-appearance of their wool-headed queen. Garbo may have preferred to be alone, but she always turned up at call-sheet time, even if at dawn. Barbara Stanwyck, amenable and considerate, who could put more real meaning into one lifted eyebrow than Monroe into an entire script, got it all over within one take and zero tantrums.

In 1966 an advanced case of galloping Norma Desmonditis turned up. Corinne Griffith, the famed actress who married actor Danny Scholl on Valentine's Day, 1965 asked for an annulment on the grounds the marriage was never consummated. Frail Danny collapsed on the witness stand, but the highlight came when Corinne Griffith (who indisputably was Corinne Griffith) said that she had been merely a stand-in and had assumed the identity of Corinne Griffith when Corinne Griffith had died. In 1966 Corinne Griffith was seventy-one years old and her non-consummated mate forty-four. The "stand-in" said she was "approximately fifty-one." The insanity of this case, in which inveterate lying-about-age became destruction of identity, has never been equalled.

The embodiment of goodness, Judge Hardy (Lewis Stone), dies from a heart attack while chasing a gang of boys throwing rocks at his Beverly Hills home. Dazzling Jayne Mansfield, her career on the skids, crashes to oblivion in June 1967 on a rain-slicked

← Marilyn's Big Sleep

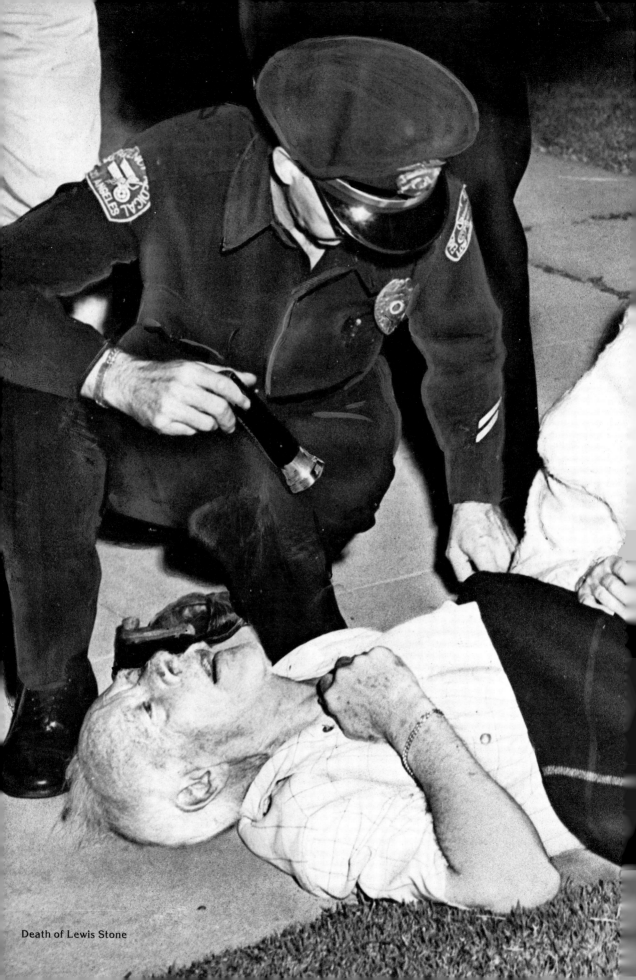

Death of Lewis Stone

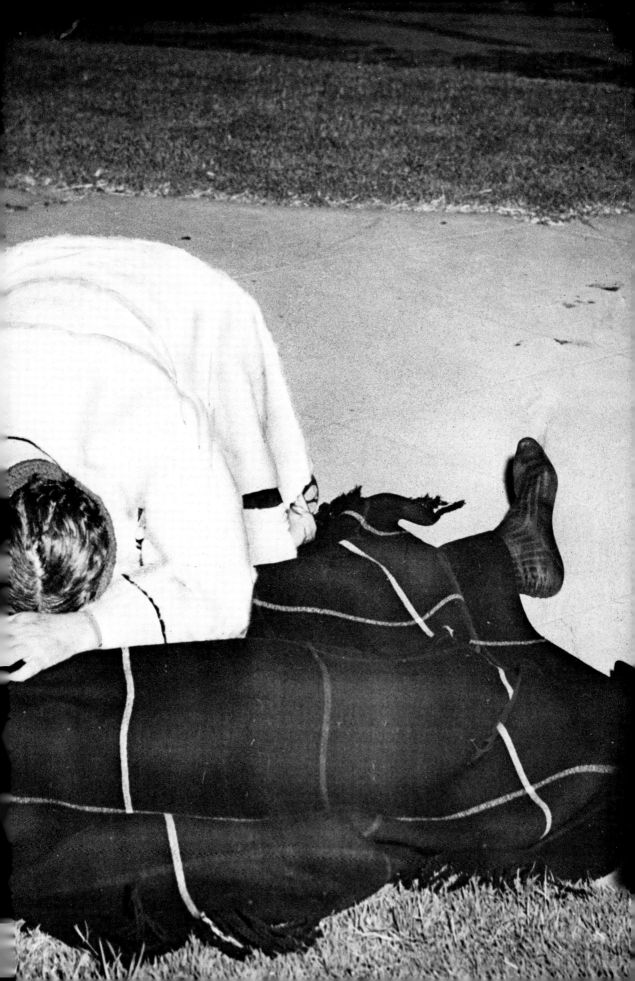

Death of Jayne Mansfield

highway. Former child actors meet sticky ends: Bobby Driscoll OD's on Methedrine; Carl "Alfalfa" Switzer is shot to death in a dope burn. Montgomery Clift and Robert Walker meet self-willed ends.

Ramon Novarro's ghastly death by beating in 1968 brought to mind the bizarre crimes of Hollywood's past.

Here was a man dying, as he had lived, extravagantly, choked in his own blood — the lead Art Deco dildo which Valentino had given him forty-five years earlier thrust down his throat. Two dumb beasts, hustler brothers from Chicago, Paul and Tom Ferguson, chose October 31, Halloween, to play Death Angels for the sixty-nine-year-old Ben Hur. All the boys wanted was his petty cash — $5000 — which they'd heard from other hustler bums that Novarro kept hidden in his Hollywood Hills home. They tore the place apart, ripping to pieces the mementoes of his long career, which meant nothing to the greedy cretins. Souvenirs drenched in blood, like Lou Tellegen's after his hara-kiri.

But Dr. Cyclops' suicide in 1968 was more Old Hollywood. In dying, Albert Dekker decided to let it all hang out and prove that he was Mr. Kink of All Time, the role he'd played in real life and the only one he believed in. For his

Novarro ↑   Paul and Tom Ferguson on trial ↑   Novarro's body is removed from his home →

284

last role, the sixty-two-year-old character actor chose his favorite private garb, women's silk lingerie. He carefully printed in crimson lipstick on his gone-to-flab anatomy his final notices, all of them unfavorable. Then, in delicious schadenfreude, he bound himself, and managed to hang himself, even as his favorite handcuffs locked on his wrists for all time. This time, he played the game alone, in his Hollywood bathroom. He had delivered himself of his disillusionment to critic Ward Morehouse, eight years before, reflecting on his forty-year career:"The theater is a horrible place in which to make a living. They sit you on the shelf for years. They take you off and brush you off and later you have to find your way back to that shelf." These sentiments betray the dedication of the true bondage fan, even in regard to his profession. Dekker left no messages, beyond the breathtaking tableau, yet another odd still life for Dr. Noguchi's collection.

George Sanders' suicide in a Spain drained of all Romance was nude, lonely, elderly of soul. His note held the proper professional cynic's touch: it was goodbye to the Sweet Cesspool, life itself. He was bored with every bit of it.

The '69 Tate massacre was not Old Hollywood. What befell the red house on Cielo Drive resembled the devastation caused by a jet plane crash: the Bad Ship Lollipop piloted by Uncle Sugar. Charlie Manson — programmed puppet, deus ex-garbage can. Wasted lives make waste, not tragedy. This was the Benedict Canyon where Paul Bern shot himself; his noble shade now has mixed company.

Judy's self-snuff took place in a locked London bathroom. MGM's Amphetamine Annie really made it at last after so many attempts — pills, wrist slashings years before in her Hollywood bathroom, hack hack with broken glass. Dorothy died

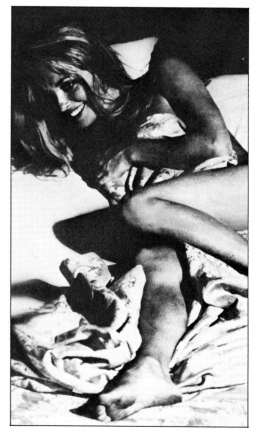

Albert Dekker: Kinky suicide ↑   **Sharon Tate: Massacred** ↑   **Blood on Sharon's doorstep** →

seated on the "loo," but this was no Over-the-Rainbow trip. Fully dressed, crouched over as if in meditation, her face a welter of blood, an Aztec mask. She was hundreds of years old, the oldest star ever, if you count emotional years, the toll they take, dramas galore for a dozen lifetimes. She was "She," who had stepped into the Flame once too often.

They have restored the Hollywood Sign, just the first nine letters — H O L L Y W O O D. They have strengthened the supporting poles and repainted the tin. By accident or design, the remaining four original letters (L A N D) have been junked or have rotted away. The thirteenth letter, the final D is no longer there to tempt a new Peg Entwistle. New generations at Hollywood High are not even aware that the monolith on Mount Lee ever spelled anything more than the name of the smog-shrouded town which lies below: a town that today is soooo Miami Beach. TACK-EEEEEE.

Judy: Old, old, old →

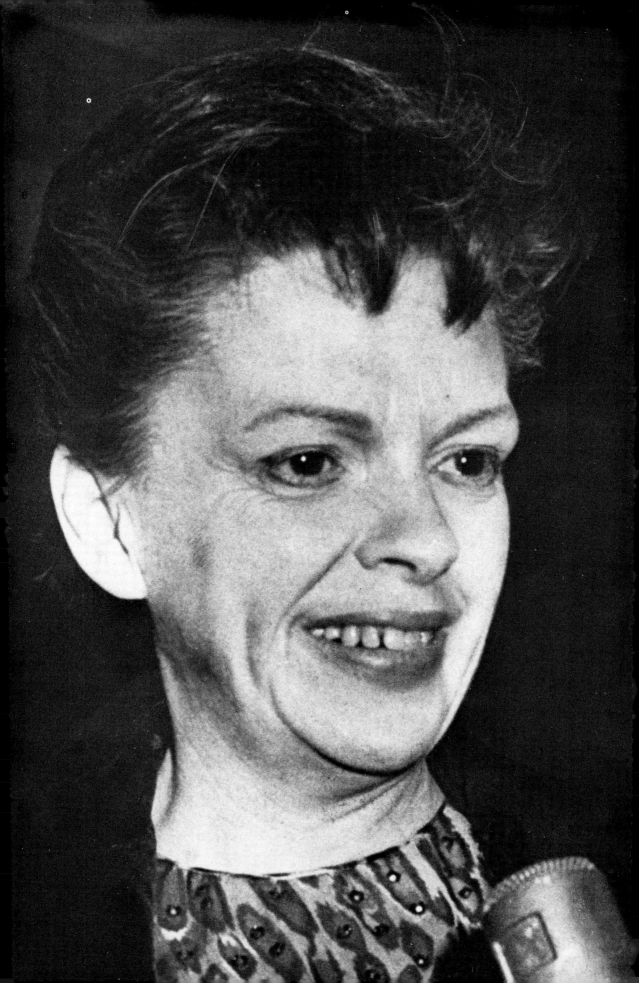

In need of repair: The Hollywood Sign

On the empty stages of Columbia, where Harry Cohn's electronic ears were once perked, they play tennis these days. (Outside on Gower Gulch, the tacked-on FOR SALE sign fades.) Yet, sometimes after fierce rains and winds have swept the skies clean, the Egyptian blue reappears over a still-Spanished, still-palmed plain like the Cytherean isle Catalina, discerned on the horizon on a blue ribbon, the hulking, obsolete sound stages like secretive mastabas picked out below, and we can imagine what drew the ambitious and reckless men here, an age ago.

·END OF REEL·

Cohn of Columbia ↑   White Elephants: Columbia's empty stages ↑   Tennis, anyone?

HOLLYWOOD

HE: When on the sidewalk I see —
SHE: Pardon me, but aren't you Dick Powell?
HE: Yes, I'm Dick Powell.
SHE: I wonder if you'd, do me . . . I thought maybe (<u>sob</u>) —
HE: Here, here, here — What's the matter?
SHE: Oh you wouldn't understand. Hollywood's been good to you!
HE: What do you mean?
SHE: Oh, I guess it's an old story . . . There was a beauty contest in Little Rock.
I won it. Came to Hollywood to win fame. Instead — I'm on Hollywood
Boulevard at two in the morning. And no place to go. (<u>sob</u>)
HE: Oh, poor kid. Why don't you go home? I'd be glad to help —
SHE: Oh I can't go home a failure. You wouldn't understand but —
HE: But what?
SHE: Well it may sound silly after all the disappointments I've had, but I know
that all I need is a break. If I could get just one real chance —
HE: Well isn't there anyone at home who misses you?
SHE: There . . . There's a boy there. He works in a garage and he's a swell guy.
He — he — wants to marry me.
HE: Well listen kid you've got more than anything <u>Hollywood</u> can offer you.
You know, there are lots of girls you envy . . . who only wish a swell guy was
waiting for <u>them</u> in Little Rock. Or anyplace else for that matter.
SHE: I guess you're right Mr. Powell. Huh — and I thought Hollywood was a
boulevard of beautiful dazzling dreams —
HE: But I'm afraid you're <u>dead</u> wrong!
(Dick Powell sings:)

I walk along the street of sorrow
The Boulevard of Broken Dreams
Where Gigolo — and Gigolette
Can take a kiss — without regret
So they forget their broken dreams
You laugh tonight and cry tomorrow
When you behold your shattered schemes,
And Gigolo — and Gigolette
Wake up and find their eyes are wet
With tears that tell of broken dreams —

Here is where you'll always find me
Always walking up and down
But I left my soul behind me
In an old Cathedral town.
The joy that you find here you borrow
You cannot keep it long it seems.
But Gigolo — and Gigolette
Still sing a song
And dream along
The Boulevard of Broken Dreams.

(Sequence excised from the 1934 Warners'
musical <u>Moulin Rouge</u> by order of Jack Warner
as "Too depressing!")

Jayne Mansfield's dead dog

·INDEX·

Ginger Rogers without makeup

· CREDITS ·

The author wishes to thank the following individuals and institutions for their generous assistance: Elliott Stein; Samson De Brier; Dan Price; Charles Higham; James Card, George C. Pratt, George Eastman House Museum of Photography; Mary Corliss, Stills Collection, Museum of Modern Art Department of Film; Charles Silver, Library, Museum of Modern Art Department of Film; Henry Langlois, Mary Meerson, Lotte Eisner, Cinémathèque Française; Camille Cook, Film Center, School of the Art Institute of Chicago; Tom Luddy, Pacific Film Archive; Sandy Brown Wyeth; Dan Faris, The Cinema Shop; Bill Brandt, Saturday Matinee; The Memory Shop; Movie Star News; Fabiano Canosa; Mark Stephenson, Cinemabilia; Photoplay; Anton Szandor LaVey; the late Bob Pike; the late James Whale; the late Mae Murray.

The author gratefully acknowledges permission to reprint the following: "Hollywood" by Don Blanding, reprinted by permission of Dodd, Mead Company, Inc.; "First Fig" by Edna St. Vincent Millay, from Collected Poems, Harper & Row, copyright 1922, 1950 by Edna St. Vincent Millay; Chicago Tribune editorial, "Pink Powder Puffs," reprinted, courtesy of the Chicago Tribune; "Boulevard of Broken Dreams" (Harry Warren-Al Dubin), © 1933 Remick Music Corp., copyright renewed, all rights reserved, used by permission of Warner Bros. Music.

Photographs:
Museum of Modern Art Department of Film: ii, viii–ix, x–xi, 2, 4–5, 10–11, 12 (top), 13, 17, 19, 46 (left and right), 48, 50–51, 53, 54 (right), 55, 72, 73, 74–75, 76 (left and right), 77, 78, 86, 89, 93 (right), 95, 96, 106, 129, 133 (left), 140–141, 153, 158 (bottom), 170, 178–179, 186–187, 243, 248, 251, 295; Bob Pike Photo Library: 7, 8, 14, 24, 35 (bottom), 40, 56, 70, 109, 124, 142 (top), 143, 182, 185 (left and right), 230, 237, 250, 265, 270 (right), 274 (top); George Eastman House Museum of Photography: 12 (bottom), 118–119, 120, 121, 122–123, 234–235, 236 (right); Samson De Brier: 54 (left), 60 (top), 68, 152 (left), 224 (left), 156 (top); Dan Price Collection: 114 (left), 133 (right), 168 (bottom), 221, 290–291; Tom Luddy Collection: 9, 90–91, 134, 158 (top); Sandy Brown Wyeth: 30, 69 (insert), 292 (bottom), 304–305; United Press International: 160, 167, 192, 196-197, 199, 238, 240, 244, 245, 247, 263, 275, 284 (top and bottom), 285, 287; New York Public Library Theater Collection: 8, 42; National Film Archive: 6; Wide World Photos: 254–255, 268, 270, 271, 276, 282–283, 287; Cinemabilia: 242; Kenneth Kendall: 306; Bill Ray, Time-Life Picture Agency: 126; Dan Faris: 146 (bottom), 289, 301, 302; Art Institute of Chicago: 188; other illustrations from the Kenneth Anger Collection.

Tyrone Power's grave

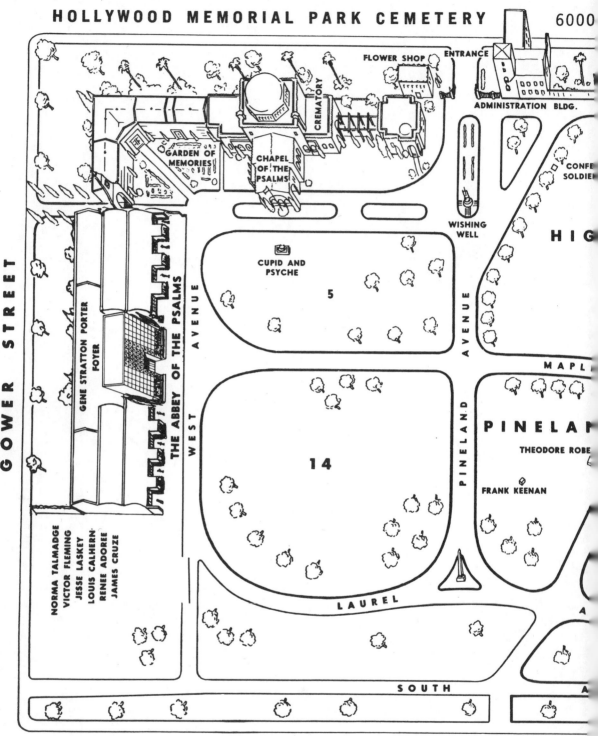

HOLLYWOOD MEMORIAL PARK CEMETERY 6000

GOWER STREET

FLOWER SHOP ENTRANCE
CREMATORY
ADMINISTRATION BLDG.
GARDEN OF MEMORIES
CHAPEL OF THE PSALMS
CONFE SOLDIE
WISHING WELL
HIG
GENE STRATTON PORTER FOYER
THE ABBEY OF THE PSALMS
WEST AVENUE
CUPID AND PSYCHE
5
AVENUE
MAPL
14
PINELAND
PINELAND
THEODORE ROBE
FRANK KEENAN
NORMA TALMADGE
VICTOR FLEMING
JESSE LASKEY
LOUIS CALHERN
RENEE ADOREE
JAMES CRUZE
LAUREL
SOUTH
A